THE
POWER
of THREE

Navigating You to a Worry-Free Retirement with Lower Taxes, Maximum Growth, and Guaranteed Income

SAMANTHA M. IRISH & KAREN E. STAWICKI

FOREWORD WRITTEN BY TOM HEGNA

Compass Financial
PUBLICATIONS

Editing, design, distribution by Bublish

Published by Compass Financial Publications

ISBN: 978-1-647048-64-8 (paperback)
ISBN: 978-1-647048-71-6 (eBook)

TABLE OF CONTENTS

FOREWORD

It's with great pleasure that I introduce you to *The Power of Three*, authored by the dynamic mother-daughter duo, Karen Stawicki and Samantha Irish. Having known these remarkable women for over twenty-five years, I've witnessed firsthand their unwavering dedication to empowering individuals to achieve financial security and peace of mind. Their collective wisdom and expertise shine through in this invaluable guide, which illuminates the path to a prosperous and worry-free retirement.

In *The Power of Three*, Karen and Samantha delve into the three essential financial pillars that form the bedrock of a secure retirement: guaranteed lifetime income, cash value life insurance, and investable assets. These pillars serve as the cornerstone of a comprehensive retirement strategy, providing a sturdy framework to weather life's uncertainties and enjoy the golden years with confidence.

At the heart of their approach lies the concept of guaranteed lifetime income, a crucial component that ensures a steady stream of income to cover basic living expenses throughout retirement. By mitigating longevity risk, market volatility, and other financial uncertainties, this pillar offers a sense of stability and security that is invaluable in today's uncertain economic landscape.

Furthermore, Karen and Samantha underscore the pivotal role of cash value life insurance in safeguarding against unforeseen events and enhancing financial flexibility. Beyond its traditional role as a safety net, life insurance can unlock tax-free income in retirement and provide a tax-efficient means of transferring wealth to future generations, affording individuals the freedom to enjoy their wealth with confidence and peace of mind.

Of course, no retirement plan is complete without the third pillar of investable assets, which serve as the engine of growth and prosperity. By carefully managing liquidity, taxes, and inflation, individuals can harness the power of their investments to build wealth and ensure a comfortable standard of living well into retirement.

In *The Power of Three*, Karen and Samantha go beyond mere theory, offering real-world case studies that illustrate the tangible benefits of their approach. These stories serve as a testament to the transformative impact of their principles, showcasing how individuals from all walks of life have achieved financial security and peace of mind under their guidance.

Their insights are further validated by a recent Ernst & Young Whitepaper, which underscores the importance of a balanced retirement portfolio consisting of 30% income annuities, 30% cash value life insurance, and 40% investments. *The Power of Three* distills this complex research into actionable strategies that anyone can implement to achieve financial prosperity in retirement.

In a world inundated with financial advice, *The Power of Three* stands out for its simplicity, clarity, and practicality. Karen and Samantha's writing style is straightforward and accessible, making complex financial concepts easy to understand and implement. Whether you're just embarking on your retirement journey or seeking to optimize your existing plan, this book is an indispensable resource that will guide you every step of the way.

In closing, I commend Karen Stawicki and Samantha Irish for their invaluable contribution to the field of retirement planning. *The Power of Three* is more than just a book; it's a roadmap to financial freedom and peace of mind. May it serve as a guiding light on your journey to a fulfilling and prosperous retirement.

Warm regards,

Tom Hegna

Tom Hegna is an economist, author, and retirement expert. He has been an incredibly popular industry speaker for many years and is considered by many to be THE retirement income expert. As a former First Vice President at New York Life, retired Lieutenant Colonel, and economist, Tom has delivered over 5,000 seminars on his signature "Paychecks and Playchecks" retirement approach, helping baby boomers and seniors retire the "optimal" way. Tom specializes in creating simple and powerful retirement solutions and has been featured in, Forbes, FOX Business, WSJ: Money Rates, *and many other leading publications.*[1]

---

[1]   www.tomhegna.com, "About," Tom Hegna, 2011–2024.

INTRODUCTION

Despite what any financial advisor, analyst, or nosy in-law tells you—there is just no way to predict exactly what your financial future will look like. Thankfully, there are steps you can take today to shift the tide in your favor. The good news? You've already taken the first step—picking up *The Power of 3*— and are well on your way to planning for your ideal retirement while also safeguarding your financial future from the mistakes that can derail even the best of us. This book will put you in the driver's seat so, as the world evolves, you remain in a position to steer your success!

The key to being in control of your retirement success? *The Power of 3*.

When most people start investing, they think the stock market is the right place to be—and if time is on their side, then they would be correct. But that isn't always the case. When we meet our clients for the first time, 90 to 95% of them are almost exclusively invested in the market.

The problem is that relying on the market alone is as risky as putting all your eggs in one basket—and everyone knows that's a bad idea. However, the problem is greater than "one basket." I want you to think about taking a ride on a unicycle. If you are young and agile, falling off isn't a problem, but the older you get, the smarter it would be to take the same ride on a tricycle. The same is true when you think about your financial journey. The older you get, the more stability and guarantees you want that you will make it to your destination.

The good news is that there are plenty of different baskets for your eggs. The even better news is that as you read *The Power of 3*, we will help you decide how to create stability and guarantees for you and your unique financial plans.

Who We Are

The two-person team behind *The Power of 3* includes myself, Samantha (Sam) Irish, and my mother and business partner, Karen Stawicki. We officially became partners ten years ago after I finally fulfilled my promise to join her. Quick backstory: I promised my mom I would go into business with her when I was 11, after years of financial talks around the dinner table. What 11-year-old says she wants to grow up and sell life insurance? Well, fast forward a few years, a few careers, and a few states: we were finally both living in the same place, and we were finally able to make her dreams a reality. Of course, I was always her exit strategy but also the succession plan for our clients.

Over the years, we began to specialize in risk-free retirement strategies for which there truly are "no bad days." You can turn on the TV in any market situation, no matter who is president, with confidence your plan will work. Our mission is to make complex financial strategies simple while also giving our clients the confidence to make financial decisions in light of an ever-changing future. We have spent years gathering important insight into what works and what doesn't in the realm of planning for retirement—and rather than keeping all that information exclusive to our clients, we decided to compile it into an easy-to-follow book that all sorts of people can access and benefit from.

That was when *The Power of 3* was born. We thank you for picking up this book and sincerely hope it helps you plan for a more reliable financial future and retirement. Because we can't offer you the hands-on experience we would offer a personal client, we would love to invite you to sit in on what a typical first-time meeting with us looks like. This will give you insight into how we forecast financial speed bumps, diagnose flawed retirement plans, and curate strategies on a case-by-case basis. In chapter 1, we will begin with Tom Murphy, whose case study perfectly breaks down the concept of *The Power of 3*. Then, throughout the rest of the book, we will invite you to observe other client case studies that will further enhance your understanding of the topics discussed in this book. At the end of every chapter, you'll find a chapter wrap-up section with thought-provoking questions and key points meant to facilitate your understanding of the material. You can also reference the glossary at the end of the book for any unfamiliar terms. We provide references for further study, including links to our seminars, courses, and even a one-on-one meeting with Karen and me as a brand-new client, if that's what you'd like. For now, let's dive in!

CHAPTER 1

THE POWER OF 3

It has always been our mission to simplify the more complicated aspects of money management as much as humanly possible, allowing our clients the ability to enhance their financial literacy in easy-to-digest, bite-size pieces. This desire is what ultimately led us to discovering *The Power of 3*—the three financial pillars we believe contribute to a successful retirement.

As noted in the previous section, we would like to invite you to a few client meetings—or case studies, if you will—that will help you better understand the material being discussed. In this chapter, you will learn about *The Power of 3* by sitting in on our very first case study. (Don't forget to take a few minutes to engage with the wrap-up section at the end of the chapter.)

The Power of 3
Case Study: Tom Murphy

A few summers ago, we met with a new client by the name of Tom. He had been saving for forty-plus years and believed he had listened to enough advice along the way and had created a good strategy for retirement. As usual, we had sat down together in our office's meeting room, a fresh Compass Financial notepad and a pot of hot coffee at the ready as we began the job of rolling up our sleeves and reviewing Tom's retirement plans.

He took a sip of his coffee and smiled at us. "Thanks for seeing me today, Karen and Sam," he began, eyes bright behind the silver-rimmed glasses that matched the color of his hair almost perfectly. "I'm planning to retire in three years and figured I'd reach out for a second opinion to make sure my plan is solid."

Karen returned his smile. "Of course, Tom. We're happy to review your current strategy. Before we dive into the numbers, tell us a little about yourself. What does retirement look like for you?"

"Well, after forty years of working as an X-ray technician in the health-care industry, I'm hoping it will at least be relaxing."

I laughed, mentally reading the exhaustion on Tom's face.

He leaned in. "You know, I stayed with one company for almost thirty years to be able to create a small pension. Sarah and I have two grown children and just found out we will become grandparents next year."

"Tom," I asked, "do you like to travel? Do you have any hobbies?"

"I love golf and fishing, but we've never been able to travel much because of my demanding work schedule. I'm hoping to change that once I'm officially retired."

"It sounds like you have a pretty good idea of what you want to do in retirement," I commented. "Good for you. Not everyone we meet with has a clear idea."

"Do you know, on an annual basis, how much it will cost to live the type of retirement you're planning?" Karen asked.

"I'm projecting I'll need about $150,000 per year once I retire."

"Wonderful," I said. "And where do you see that money coming from in your strategy?"

"I currently have $1,500,00 in my retirement accounts, and I've been getting about an 8% return, on average," Tom responded, referring to a notebook filled with notes and numbers. "So I'm assuming I can withdraw about $80,000 a year from those accounts. Plus, I have my pension, which is $40,000 per year, and another $30,000 from our combined Social Securities. That gets us to $150,000."

Tom had a great big smile, but it faded as he saw the concern on our faces. I nodded at Karen, prompting her to respond.

"Tom, when taken at face value, your math is solid," she said carefully, using the same approach we'd used many times before with clients who had fallen into similar traps. "But I have a question: Will you withdraw income from your retirement accounts *every* year or just the years when the market performs well?"

"My plan was to take it every year. Is that not a good plan?"

"Since you can't control fluctuations in the market's performance, you have to plan for down years. For example, if you're taking out $80,000 when the market is only performing at 3% or is flat—or, God forbid, when it's down—then your math starts to fall apart."

At this, Tom's face started to get a little pale. Karen quickly got to her point.

"You risk drawing your assets too aggressively to keep meeting your retirement needs over the long term, which probably isn't the safest retirement strategy. Does that make sense?"

"Have you ever considered a negative market?" I asked.

Tom wasn't smiling anymore. "Honestly, no. . . . I just assumed it would be like when I was growing the money. When the market is down, you sit and wait it out. Are you saying I shouldn't be invested in the market?"

"Absolutely not," I stated emphatically. "The market can be your friend, even in bad years. You just don't want to rely *only* on the market. You need to balance things out to insulate your retirement assets from too much risk."

"That makes sense, Sam. But how do I do that?"

"We're big believers in *The Power of 3*," I began, reaching for a clean sheet of paper to draw a diagram representing the philosophy. "There are three pieces to your retirement we need you to focus on. First is income. Currently, your income is provided by your paycheck from work. When you retire, you need your assets to create a paycheck for you."

I drew a circle around the words *guaranteed income* on the clean sheet of paper, adding three lines branching out from that circle, representing different income streams. I added *Social Security*, *pension*, and *annuities* to the lines.

"Second, we want you to think about liquidity and safety," I went on, drawing a circle around the words *liquidity* and *safety*. "This second piece protects you from timing risk. This means the potential for missing out on a benefit to your asset because of an error in timing. For instance, leaving your money invested right before a big market crash or moving your assets to money market right before the market increases 25%.

"Lastly, you need to think about growth," I concluded, drawing a circle around the word. "It's true your paycheck grew over the years, and that was how you kept up with inflation. The same must be true when it comes to your retirement. Inflation risk is the risk that inflation will undermine an investment's returns through a decline in purchasing power. We protect against this by giving your money permission to remain invested in the market."

"Okay," Tom replied, appearing a little more optimistic. "I think I'm following you."

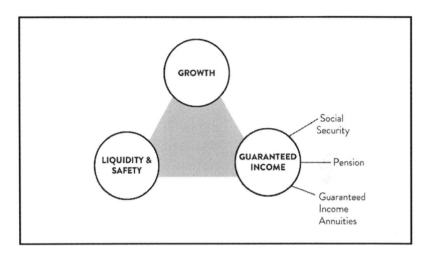

"We like to say that money has job descriptions, and your dollar can only do one job at a time. Your money can provide income, it can be safe and liquid, or it can grow," Karen added, pointing at the three circles I had drawn. "When you ask your money to do more than one task, it can't do any of the jobs well. So, for you, the first thing we need to focus on is income. I want you to think about your Social Security and pension. Can you tell me what the best thing about those two assets is?"

"Well, based on the drawing," Tom said, looking for confirmation, "is it that my Social Security and pension are guaranteed forms of income I can rely on?"

"That is exactly right, Tom," I replied, refilling my mug of coffee. Tom grinned, holding out his mug for a refill as well, which I happily offered. "Think about it. Every year—no matter what the market is doing or who is president or how well you slept last night—$70,000 is being deposited into your account. That's almost half your desired income. That's a big deal!"

Tom chuckled, nodding. It was clear he hadn't fully considered how significant those two assets were. Like many of our clients, he had always been more focused on growing his retirement accounts. This is one of the many common missteps people make in retirement planning—but the good news is that when caught early on, this isn't nearly as detrimental as it could be. In fact, this misstep is easily reversed.

"Now," Karen went on to add, "we want to make sure that 100% of your guaranteed expenses are covered with guaranteed income, like your pension and Social Security. This is how we make sure you are not exposed to what is called longevity risk. We know your goal is $150,000 a year in retirement, but that includes the ability to travel with your family and have a little fun. Do you know what your guaranteed expenses will be on an annual basis?"

Tom had never done the math, but with a quick review of his budget, we were able to determine that he would need approximately $120,000—approximately $10,000 a month—of guaranteed income for his guaranteed expenses. This total would cover his mortgage, car payments, food, memberships, et cetera.

This introduces another common misstep in retirement planning. It's important to identify both income and expenses that are guaranteed. This is an easy way to map out what is a *want* and what is a *need*.

After mapping out Tom's guaranteed income and expenses, Karen proceeded to discuss the market in more detail. "Tom," she began, "remember earlier when we discussed the risk of relying on withdrawing money from the market every year? I want to explain that a little better. You see, your plan of taking $80,000 from your money in the market means you are taking almost a 6% withdrawal from your investment portfolio. This is risky. The average rate people believe they can take is 4%, but even at 4%, there is a 70%–80% chance of running out of money."

"Is there a rate you would recommend?" Tom asked, brows furrowed. "Would you recommend something less than 4%?"

"Yes, actually," I interjected. "The bulletproof rate is 2%."

"Two percent?" Tom asked, surprised. "Is that so?"

"At 2%, we could only generate another $30,000 a year for you in retirement. Unfortunately, that doesn't get you to the amount you need to cover your guaranteed expenses," Karen chimed in. "Plus, a systematic withdrawal is never guaranteed anyway. Instead, we want to introduce you to a guaranteed life-time income annuity, a financial product that pays out a fixed stream of payments to an individual. A moment ago, Sam referred to longevity risk. Do you know what that is?"

Tom shook his head, taking a sip of coffee. "I think I've got an idea, but I'm not sure."

"Longevity risk is the danger of living too long," Karen answered. "This is also considered a risk multiplier because it makes all the other factors worse. By creating guaranteed income to cover your guaranteed expenses, we make sure you will never run out of money before heartbeats." (Sorry, when it comes to retirement and finances, we must talk about death.) "What is your knowledge or experience with annuities, Tom?"

"I'm not too familiar, but I thought you had to give up control of your money. I've heard annuities are bad," Tom said. He crossed his arms slowly and leaned back in his chair. "I've also heard about how expensive they are, and my neighbor lost a bunch of money when he surrendered one. I don't think annuities are for me."

Karen and I briefly made eye contact at this moment. This was not an uncommon response whenever we brought up annuities to a new client.

"The truth is, Tom, that just like you, annuities have evolved and grown over time. You wouldn't want someone judging you today based on your 17-year-old self, right?" Everybody chuckled a bit at that. A lot of change takes place between 17 years old and near-retirement age. "Annuities today give the investor a lot more control and choices. The most important characteristic about annuities, though, is that, besides Social Security and a pension, they are the only other form of guaranteed income."

At this, Tom's eyes lit up a bit. "I like the sound of *guaranteed*."

"Remember, Tom," I added, "in order to cover your guaranteed expenses with guaranteed income, we need to use one of three solutions. You can't get more Social Security—you've already paid into the system to build that. And you can't get another pension—most companies don't even offer them anymore, and you had to work for your current employer for thirty years to build the one you have. So the only other way for us to cover that expenses gap of $50,000 annually is with a guaranteed income annuity. Would you be willing to see how that works and how much it would 'cost' to create that income stream for yourself?"

After further discussion, we determined that in order to generate the additional $50,000 of Tom's guaranteed income, he would need to reposition $750,000 from his $1,500,000 in IRAs in the annuity.

"I never thought I'd say this, but let's do it," Tom said, clearly surprised by his own reaction. "I feel really good about doing more with less, so to speak—and I'll still be able to keep $750,000 in my IRA. Let's use the annuity to fill the remaining guaranteed income I need. I love the idea of $120,000 a year guaranteed coming to me and my wife. However, I do have one question: Once that is covered, can I expect to get the discretionary $30,000 from my investments? Based on the math before, I don't think I can get $30,000 annually from $750,000."

"Well, you would be right about that," Karen said frankly. "But keep in mind the three job descriptions of money—income, liquidity and safety, and growth. We have already covered income by securing your guaranteed expenses with guaranteed solutions. Now we need to address the jobs of liquidity and safety and growth. Remember, we said money can't do both if we want it to do those jobs well—which, of course, we do. To access those dollars, you need liquidity. Tom, in your opinion, where is the best place for you to get liquidity and safety?"

"That's a no-brainer—the bank," declared Tom. "But even though my bank is paying a little more today, they keep telling us interest rates are coming down, and I remember getting 'point nothing' a few years ago, so there's no way I'd want to put any portion of my retirement accounts into a bank."

"Good job, Tom," said Karen. "We don't want you to put your liquid assets into a traditional bank either. But have you heard of "The Bank of Tom"—or a 7702? Maybe you've heard of cash value life insurance? It's a strategy that many savvy investors are using to create tax-free liquid assets in retirement while maintaining a better rate of return than the banks offer."

Tom's brows furrowed. "Isn't that what banks use to secure their reserves? I always assumed it was only available to large corporations or the super wealthy."

Karen and I glanced at one another, exchanging an encouraging laugh. "Tom," I went on, "I've got great news for you: the only requirements are earned income and your health. Our recommendation would be to use a portion of your retirement accounts, distribute the income strategically to pay as little tax as legally possible, and build a cash value life insurance policy, combined with the remaining invested assets, for you to generate the income necessary to fund your travel and fun in retirement."

"The solution of cash value life insurance is not only great for your liquidity and safety," Karen added, tapping the diagram I'd drawn on a sheet of paper earlier, "but it also protects against two more retirement risks: long-term care risk and risk of death. Long-term care risk is the risk of needing services to help meet both the medical and nonmedical needs of chronic illness or disability when you cannot care for yourself for a long period of time. According to the National Clearinghouse for long-term care information,[2] a person's lifetime risk of needing LTC services in their lifetime is one out of two—that's a 50% risk. As age increases, so does the likelihood of needing care. The good news is that a lot of permanent life insurance solutions include LTC coverage. So, basically, it's long-term care if you need it, life insurance if you don't."

"Plus," I went on, "the presence of life insurance gives you permission to spend your other assets differently because you

---

[2] "Basic Needs," LongTermCare.gov, US Department of Health and Human Services, last modified August 2, 2021, https://acl.gov/ltc/basic-needs.

know, in the event of your premature death, the asset bag gets filled back up with your death benefit, and the party keeps going for your wife and children."

"Wow! I knew life insurance was a good thing, but I always figured you had to die to benefit, and if I was dead, I wasn't really benefiting," Tom said sheepishly.

(A quick note: we hear this a lot, and while you'd think Tom would be fully aware of the benefit to his family, even if he was gone, most people believe their family could turn to other solutions in their absence or would benefit more from their investing the money in the market.)

"But don't forget," Karen chimed in, "to complete this plan, you would use a portion of the remaining $750,000 in your retirement accounts to purchase cash value life insurance, which will give you access to the $30,000 a year if you need it for your wants. In years when the market does great, you take your remaining income needs from your investments; in the years the market underperforms, you have this tax-free account in life insurance to give you the income until the market comes back.

"Remember, because of the presence of the cash value life insurance, you now have permission to stay invested in the market with the rest of your retirement account, thus giving you the last piece of the job description: growth. Tom, you should be really proud of yourself. You did everything right to get to this point in retirement, and your plan might have worked, but in our opinion, it left you exposed to too many risks. With just a few adjustments and really giving each of your dollars a specific job to do, you will be able to eliminate those risks and create the confident retirement you walked in here hoping for. Is there anything else you are worried about, or should we get started?"

"Let's do this!" Tom said with a renewed sense of excitement.

The reason we chose to invite you into Tom's story particularly is because this is a great example of what we've seen most during our time in business: a well-intended client has a plan for retirement that might work, but they have a lot of exposure to risk. Risks are the trapdoor of retirement; one minute you are walking along and everything is going great and then, bam!

Remember what we promised you at the beginning of this section: while we don't have a crystal ball, our goal is to show you how you can eliminate and influence these risks so you enter retirement with your hands on the controls.

Ready to dive into the details of how *The Power of 3* works? Us too!

Chapter Wrap-Up

Make a list of your predicted guaranteed expenses below. We'll get you started with the expenses we see most often:

- Mortgage payment
- Car payments
- Food
- Insurance (home and auto)
- Taxes

Now, make a list of your guaranteed income sources. Again, there are only three, so how much can you expect from each source:

- Social Security
- Pension
- Guaranteed income annuity

What is the total amount of your guaranteed expenses? And will your guaranteed income cover those expenses? If not, brainstorm a few options to cover those expenses, or simply bookmark this section and return to it after you've finished reading this book. (We hope by the end, you'll be able to answer this question with more confidence!)

Finally, consider these questions:

1. Have you considered what will happen if you live longer than expected?

2. Have you thought about how market volatility could affect your income streams?
3. Could your income streams decrease as you get older?
4. What is the job you are currently asking your money to do?

CHAPTER 2

GUARANTEED INCOME ANNUITIES

M any people think a successful retirement is based on money—the bigger the dollar amount, the bigger the opportunity for a happy retirement. That's not quite true. What's more important is what you *do* with those dollars.

Our clients Bill and Stacey are a perfect example. They had worked hard for many years to save $800,000 and thought they were ready to retire. They were referred to us by another client, and when we first met them, they asked us to review their portfolio to make sure everything was in place for the big transition. Unfortunately, our review revealed several big problems.

Annuities
Case Study: Bill and Stacey White

I remember that meeting clearly. It was late summer, and the Charleston humidity was low. In celebration of the great weather, we'd made a pitcher of fresh-squeezed lemonade for our clients.

Both Bill and Stacey poured themselves a glass as we sat down for our meeting.

It was clear that Bill and Stacey were expecting Karen and me to give them the go-ahead to retire; they were all smiles as we sat down and opened their portfolio.

"Bill and Stacey, after reviewing your financial documents, it doesn't look like you have enough money to retire on your own," I began. I recall wanting to get the hard part over with so we could move on to brainstorming solutions as soon as possible. As predicted, their expressions immediately shifted from hope to concern. "But don't worry," I said with a smile. "We have a few ideas that we think will help."

The pair perked up a bit. Bill's brows raised as he said, "We're all ears."

"We suggest placing a portion of your savings into a guaranteed income annuity," Karen added, pulling out a printed breakdown of what this might look like. "Not only will it provide the potential for growth, but it will also guarantee you never run out of income. Does that make sense?"

"I don't think annuities are a good option for us," Stacey interjected. "I've heard they are very costly—and *they* have control of your money. My sister had a horrible experience."

"That's not an uncommon reaction," I said. "But do you mind if we ask you a question?"

Stacey nodded.

"Are you excited about getting your Social Security?"

"Of course," Stacey replied. "That's where a third of our retirement income is coming from."

"Social Security isn't so different from annuities. To qualify for Social Security income, you gave your money to the government during your working years and let them take control for decades, and now, they are giving it back to you."

"I've never thought about it that way," Stacey said, brows furrowed.

She glanced at Bill, who was prompted to add, "That makes a lot of sense, and we really want to retire now, but aren't there really high fees with annuities?"

"There are fees, but they are actually very low. You see, annuities have changed significantly over the years. Today, there are more consumer benefits, such as reduced costs, lower risks, multiple income streams, and more control."

We continued to discuss different types of annuities. There are annuities that focus on growth, but there are also annuities whose goal is to create income. Bill and Stacey didn't need to focus on growing their assets in retirement but rather on making sure they could count on that money on an annual basis. As we discussed in Tom's story, we shared how, in retirement, they could change the job description of those dollars from growth to income.

"Thank you for taking the time to explain all the differences and reasons this annuity would be the right fit for our situation. We can clearly see the benefit of this addition to our portfolio, and it makes sense," Bill stated. "But before we agree, can you explain how the annuity company can make this guarantee?"

"I'm glad you asked," I said. Honestly, this is one way we know a client is really invested in a solution: they ask follow-up questions, even when they think it's a good recommendation. "Income annuities work by converting a lump sum of money (or multi-year annual contributions) into a guaranteed stream of income that is paid out over a specified period, usually the rest of the investors' lives. By leveraging their expertise in managing longevity risk, life insurance companies combine the premiums coming in with income going out for annuity contracts, plus lump sums coming in from annuity purchases against lump sum distributions for insurance death benefits."

"Let's not complicate things," chimed in Karen. "Ultimately, the life insurance company is a master at balancing money in and money out to guarantee their solutions."

"Impressive," Bill agreed, sipping his lemonade. "But one more question before we move forward: Can you give me a clearer definition of what an annuity is, just to make sure we fully understand?"

"Of course," Karen said. "Annuities are contracts between you and an insurance company that require the insurer to make payments to you over time—either immediately or in the future. You buy an annuity by making either a single payment or a series of payments."

"We'll do it," Stacey said after a quick glance at Bill, who smiled. "We avoided annuities before because of the rumored risks and costs, but the priority is guaranteed income throughout retirement, and this feels like the best option."

That afternoon, we ended up balancing Bill and Stacey's retirement portfolio by including two annuities—one for each of them—to support their need for guaranteed income. At the time, we chose specific annuities whose payouts would continue to rise as the market increased. As we mentioned earlier in the book, annuities are ever evolving, but in 2024, the best options give the buyer control over the payout start date, single or joint payouts, increasing or level income, and typically, a bonus to their initial premium.

Every retirement portfolio is essentially striving to do one thing—prepare for both the expected and the unexpected. This means studying the science of life. Variables such as cost of living, lifestyle choices, and guaranteed income and expenses are relatively easy to work around as far as variables go. However, there is one variable nobody can predict, and it just so happens to drastically affect the success of your retirement plan. We'll get into that with our next case study.

Longevity Risk
Case Study: Robert Knight

The purpose of this book is to take a relatively complicated topic—retirement portfolio planning—and break it down into bite-size, digestible pieces. For this reason, we have kept the material as light as possible, focusing on the predictable variables one typically encounters during their time in retirement.

However, it is time now to discuss a subject that is slightly darker and slightly harder to predict but affects the success of one's retirement more than possibly any other variable. We're talking now about longevity risk.

There are many risks associated with retirement—market risk, timing risk, withdrawal rate risk, inflation risk, deflation risk, risk of death, and risk of long-term care. But the biggest risk by far is longevity risk. Living a long time is wonderful. Funding a long life, however, can be challenging—especially if you haven't planned for it. That is why we say that longevity risk is a risk multiplier.

This takes us to our next case study subject. Robert was a single man who had made it his goal to run two marathons a year. To describe him as *healthy* would be an understatement, but his health wasn't just a byproduct of his lifestyle; it was also coded into his genetics, as his family had a history of longevity.

When we first met with Robert, it was on the cusp of spring 2019. Almost overnight, the world went from the black-and-white monochrome of winter to the explosive bright green and pollen-coated yellow of an early spring. Robert arrived a few minutes early, wearing running gear that suggested he'd made the trip on foot or by bicycle. After a few minutes of getting acquainted, we got straight down to business.

"Robert, you have a wonderful family history of longevity," I started off, reviewing the orientation paperwork we have every new client fill out. In that paperwork, he listed parents who lived well into their nineties.

Robert nodded, smiling. "We live a long time in our family."

"Yes, I can see that." I set his paperwork down. "Have you considered how that will affect your retirement planning?"

"Honestly, I just figured I would remain invested in the stock market. It's my understanding that that's where I can get the best returns. If my money is growing, I should be able to keep taking income, regardless of my age, right?"

"That is true," Karen added. "But it is a little risky to put all your eggs in one basket."

"I agree, and honestly, I hate it," Robert admitted, shaking his head. "I check the market daily, I'm constantly reading investment articles, and I'm always wondering if I should be making a move. It's stressful, and it's almost becoming a full-time job."

"I bet you didn't think you'd work for forty-seven years as a project manager just to retire and become a stockbroker," I added, and we all enjoyed a laugh.

But it didn't take long for Robert's expression to become serious again. "The truth is, I do have a few concerns regarding a longer lifespan. Obviously, I do want to live a long time, but my mom ended up getting dementia at 76 and required part-time care from that point on, which wasn't cheap. When my dad got too old to look after my mom, they both ended up having to go into an assisted-living facility to receive full-time care around the clock."

"Out of curiosity," I went on to inquire, "did either of your parents plan their retirement around receiving long-term care?"

"No, they didn't. They barely had any retirement at all." Robert's lips pursed, a solemn expression taking over his face. "I suppose that's why I'm here. I want to make sure I am as prepared as possible in my later years."

"You've made a good decision in meeting with us today, Robert. The risk of needing long-term care is actually on the rise. The latest statistic states that 70% of adults aged 65 years and older are likely to require this level of support[3] at some point, and, as you know, it isn't cheap."

---

[3] "How Much Care Will You Need?" LongTermCare.gov, US Department of Health and Human Services, accessed March 2023, https://acl.gov/ltc/basic-needs/how-much-care-will-you-need.

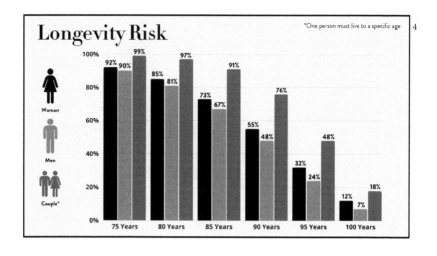

Longevity risk is the possibility that you will live longer than you expect, and as a result, you may outlive your savings. This is the biggest fear for most retirees, as most do not have a steady stream of pension income from their employer or enough other guaranteed income sources to rely on. You may have saved enough money to last for twenty years of retirement, but if you end up living for twenty-five or thirty years after retiring, you may run out of money.

Also, if you retire at 65 but then die at age 68, it doesn't matter if the stock market falls 3,000 points. It doesn't matter if you were withdrawing 10% per year or if you forgot to buy a long-term care policy—you didn't live long enough for it to matter. Now, if you live to be 85, 90, or 95, the risk of needing long-term care could be catastrophic. If we only knew the exact date you were going to die, planning would be so much easier.

---

[4]   "*The Power of 3* Masterclass." YouTube video, 5:26. Posted by Navigate Your Wealth, March 7, 2023. https://youtu.be/J4XWHhxvUCw

"How do you suggest I go about preparing for the risk of long-term care?" Robert asked us, face riddled with worry. "Is there anything I can do?"

"Of course," Karen replied, smiling encouragingly. "Even though we can't predict when we'll die, we can make an educated guess. Your family tends to have long lifespans, so we'll plan your retirement around the assumption that you will live a long time too."

"The way we address the risk of long-term care is with mortality credits," I added, pushing a sheet of paper with more information on the subject across the table. Robert put on his glasses and gave it a look. "Mortality credits are an innovative insurance-industry vehicle that uses a pool of annuity contributions to pay those who survive longer with funds from those who pass earlier. It uses the power of collective investing to provide higher and more predictable income for the group than could be achieved outside the pool. It's also a powerful portfolio risk stabilizer."

Mortality Credits

In the '80s and '90s, to prepare a proper retirement for a client, the industry would create a diversified portfolio and do what was called a systematic withdrawal. That means we would take a certain percentage withdrawal against the portfolio each year. Back then, markets were earning double digits, so taking a 7 or 8% withdrawal from the portfolio still allowed it to grow. This all worked great . . . until it didn't.

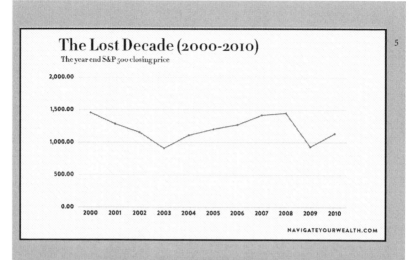

From 2000 to 2010, the market did not cooperate. It went up, sure, but it went down more often. In fact, the market ended at almost the same place in 2010 that it started in 2000. This time period is not so affectionately called "The Lost Decade."[6] Taking a 7 or 8% withdrawal from a portfolio during this decade resulted in negative returns, which was ultimately disastrous.

It quickly became apparent that we needed to find another way to provide income for our clients. We turned to guaranteed income annuities. What we discovered was that not only do annuities guarantee income and reduce market risk, but they also reduce longevity risk.

---

5   "*The Power of 3* Masterclass." YouTube video, 7:07. Posted by Navigate Your Wealth, March 7, 2023. https://youtu.be/J4XWHhxvUCw

6   "S&P 500 Historical Annual Returns," MacroTrends, accessed May 23, 2019, https://www.macrotrends.net/2526/sp-500-historical-annual-returns.

Only an insurance company can do this because of mortality credits—also known as mortality yield—which is the secret sauce of a balanced retirement portfolio. With a participating annuity, premiums paid by those who die earlier than expected contribute to the gains of the overall pool and provide a higher yield or credit to survivors than could otherwise be achieved through individual investments outside the pool.

So, how do mortality credits work? How do they provide guaranteed income?

Financial planners use computer modeling—sometimes called a Monte Carlo analysis—to calculate the probability of reaching financial goals based on assumptions. These assumptions typically account for things such as inflation-adjusted income needs and market performance.

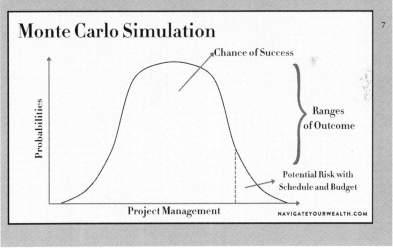

---

[7]   "*The Power of 3* Masterclass." YouTube video, 8:18. Posted by Navigate Your Wealth, March 7, 2023. https://youtu.be/J4XWHhxvUCw

For years, a 60/40 balanced approach was the mainstay of investment portfolios: investors allocated 60% to equities for capital appreciation and 40% to bonds to potentially offer income as well as risk mitigation. This approach worked well over the past decades as equities surged in a near-straight line to record highs and interest rates fell to new lows, firing up bond prices.

Robert gave me a cross-eyed look. "Any chance you can break that down in layman's terms?"

"Of course," I said, and the three of us shared a chuckle. "I shouldn't have led with such a technical breakdown of the definition. Why don't I tell you a story instead? It's a story by Tom Hegna, a globally acclaimed author in the field of economics and a dear friend of ours.

"Once upon a time, five 90-year-old ladies went on their annual vacation together. One year, one of them said, 'Hey, let's each put $100 into this box. We will tape up the box and bring it on vacation with us next year, and those of us still alive will split the money.' The other ladies agreed, and they each put $100 into the box.

"Unfortunately, the next year, one of the ladies died. So the four other ladies opened the box and split the $500. They each got $125. That was a 25% return on their $100 from just a year ago.

"I want you to think about two questions. How much of that money was invested in the stock market? Zero. What interest rate did the money earn? Zero. Well, then, how did they have a 25% return on their money in just one year? Mortality credits! They got paid mortality credits.

"So, the ladies looked at each other. They said, 'Hey, this is a pretty good deal. I think we should put the money back in the box and do it again next year.' And that is exactly what they did.

"The following year, one more lady died. Now the other three ladies split the $500. They each got $167—that was a 67% return on their original $100 of two years ago. How did they do that? Mortality credits."

"Now that makes more sense," Robert said, nodding gratefully. "How do I get in on these credits? What does one have to do to join the pool?"

"Mortality credits aren't something that you can buy or 'join,' so to speak. It's the protection that is provided through annuity solutions," Karen explained. "By pooling the money of everyone who has purchased a product from the insurance company, they create an insurance pool, ultimately sharing in the returns that come from everyone, even those who pass away early. Because of this, they are able to generate a higher rate of return than one could on their own in the market."

After incorporating an income annuity into Robert's retirement portfolio, we were able to secure the guarantee to his income, balancing his entire plan, which ultimately is our responsibility. As financial advisors, it is our job to help our clients achieve their financial retirement goals and reduce any possible risks that threaten to throw those goals out the window. We do this by helping them build and understand the benefits of a balanced approach and reviewing it on an annual or semiannual basis.

It's always enjoyable to call our clients after the first year for an annual review and talk about outcomes. Our favorite thing is to hear how much more relaxed they are than when they started their journey—often without an understanding of their options and with all their hard-earned savings in one financial bucket, like stocks.

Greg Foster was one such client.

Market Risk
Case Study: Greg Foster

We met with our long-term client Greg Foster a few years ago on a dreary fall morning. He bustled into our office wearing a heavy jacket and fleece beanie, unusual for the traditionally beautiful weather in October.

"Hi, Greg!" I said, ushering him inside. "How are you?"

"I'm doing well, Sam." He followed me into the meeting room, where Karen was waiting. A pot of hot coffee was set up at the table, along with a folder containing our notes and the portfolio we'd been working on for Greg. "Thanks for asking. How are the two of you?"

"We're great, Greg. Have a seat," Karen said, gesturing to the empty chair across from her. When the three of us got settled, she referenced her notes. "Let's go ahead and dive right in. The last time we spoke, the market performance was great, which led us to recommend you continue with your 6% distributions from your investments."

"The market has been performing so well, in fact," I chimed in, consulting my own notes, "that I recall you upping your distribution percentage to 7%. This meant taking $70,000 out last year. Is that correct?"

"Yes, that's correct. My wife and I really liked being able to travel in style last year, actually, and we're hoping to do it again."

Greg gave me an optimistic look. "The problem is that I've been watching the market, and I can't imagine this being possible."

"Unfortunately, your observations of the market are spot on, Greg." I riffled through the binder of notes in front of me, extracted a printout of the current status of the market, and handed that over to Greg. "The market dropped almost 10%. Between the drop and the large distribution you took last year, your portfolio took a hit. We may need to back off on some income this year. For that reason, I don't advise taking a 7% distribution from your portfolio again."

Despite having read the market correctly, Greg looked flabbergasted by the news. "Sam, I've got to be honest—we've really enjoyed ourselves over the last year. We've become accustomed to a certain lifestyle, so our expenses have increased. Honestly, we've come to expect that money, even though I suspected a 7% draw wouldn't be doable, given the current status of the market. Is there anything we can do?"

Client stories like these compel us to study strategies to take market volatility out of the equation. Our clients did not work hard for decades just to have to cut back on their lifestyle in retirement. These are supposed to be the glory years they worked so hard to get to. How would you feel if someone cut your monthly income in half? There had to be a better way.

Luckily, when it comes to the markets, when one financial instrument goes down, another usually goes up. When the stock market falls, interest rates typically fall too. And when interest rates fall, bonds do the opposite—their value rises.

Loosely speaking, stocks and bonds have an inverse relationship. Except in deflationary periods, investing in both typically offers a balancing mechanism within a retirement portfolio. While this correlation may be true, you are still exposing yourself to unnecessary risk. Take 2022, for example: the market dropped 19.4%, and for the first time since 1999, bonds also fell 12.9%. This meant that the safe money people had in bonds was no longer safe.

For this reason, we pair invested assets with products like annuities and life insurance, which provide tax-deferred growth and protection from market volatility. Now you're starting to see *The Power of 3* and how it can smooth out your income stream during retirement.

Sadly, people have been led to believe that if they save enough money and get a reasonable rate of return, they will be fine in retirement. Nothing could be further from the truth. The problem stems from not understanding that there are two phases of savings: accumulation and distribution. The rate of return doesn't matter when you are accumulating money; it's when you begin to withdraw your cash that the return becomes one of the most important factors to consider.

The Retirement Redzone
Case Study: Ted Cavanaugh

Ted Cavanaugh was a diligent saver who had accumulated almost $2,000,000 throughout his working years. He came to Karen and me as he became eligible for his pension and Social Security after a thirty-eight-year career.

"What brings you in today, Ted?" Karen had asked, sipping some iced tea. We had agreed to meet with Ted over lunch at his request, and with the weather as nice as it was on that day, we set up shop outside.

"I'm finding it hard to use my accumulated assets to generate income," Ted answered plainly, his mouth forming a straight line. "I've worked so hard to build the $2,000,000 that I've got set aside for retirement, and I can't bring myself to deplete it. It's my security blanket. But I'm also aware of the fact that if I don't plan on using it, I'm going to have to keep working."

"I understand, Ted," I said. "Depleting your nest egg once you enter retirement can be a hard pill to swallow."

"What if we just aggressively invest in the market to make up for the amount of money I will need to withdraw for my annual income?"

"While that works when the market does well, it can be very problematic when the market underperforms," said Karen. "Think about accumulation and distribution like rolling a snowball up and down a hill. Accumulation is like a snowball rolling downhill—it picks up snow along the way and gets bigger. It also starts to pick up speed. If the snowball is money, that feels great. In the distribution phase of your life, when you're living off the income from your investments, you're rolling the ball up the hill—it's hard to move, and snow is falling off as you push. The snowball is getting smaller, and there is no momentum."

"I understand, but I've always been successful in the market. I survived 2000 and 2010, after all, and I think I can survive this too." At this, Ted gave me a determined look. "You just have to wait it out—right, Sam?"

I steeled myself and gave it to him straight. "Ted, if you are relying on your assets to continue to grow while also providing you with income, you are asking the dollar to do two different jobs, and that doesn't work."

"This is what we refer to as the Retirement Redzone," Karen interjected smoothly, setting her tea aside to pull out the chart. "This term was coined by Prudential Insurance. Many people think that the older you are, the riskier the market is. That is not true. In reality, the riskiest time to invest your money is during the five years before retirement and the five years after. This ten-year period is when an individual's investment portfolio is most vulnerable to market volatility and other financial risks."

Retirement Redzone

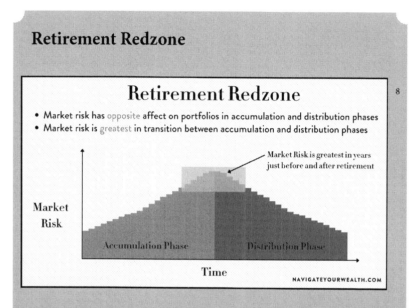

As a result of the vulnerability of the Retirement Redzone, traditional financial guidance recommends that individuals reduce their investment risk as they approach retirement and during the early years of retirement. This can mean shifting investment portfolios to more conservative, income-generating investments, such as bonds. While doing so can help minimize the impact of market volatility on retirement income, it doesn't eliminate all

---

8   "Are You in the Retirement Redzone?" Prudential Insurance Company, November 2007, https://www.prudential.com/media/system/cda/rrz/downloads/redzone_brochure.pdf.

risk. In fact, this approach can create a new risk called bond value risk. We saw this in 2022, when the stock market and the bond market both went down. By adding a third leg to the portfolio, an income component, *The Power of 3* kicks in with protection against risks in the Retirement Redzone, and its protection continues well into retirement.

Losing money in the ten-year Redzone can devastate a retirement portfolio. Think about what early or preretirement looked like in 2008, 2009, and 2010 (also known as the Great Recession) for those who had all their money in the markets. It certainly was not a story with a happy ending.

"So what do you think I should do?" Ted asked bluntly. "I'm only two years away from retirement, and I just don't feel comfortable pulling from the $2,000,000 total. I was hoping to continue letting that money grow while taking a small percentage out every year for income. You're telling me I can't do both at once?"

"Ted, do you recall us teaching you about *The Power of 3*? It's a solution we've come up with over the years, which simplifies the process of putting together a successful plan for retirement."

"Yeah, Sam, I do remember that," Ted replied. "Income, liquidity and safety, and growth."

"Those are the three pillars of a successful retirement," Karen chimed in, "but each of them has to be able to stand on its own. If you're asking your money to provide income as well as growth, what are you doing?"

Ted laughed a little, shaking his head. "Asking it to do two things at once."

"Exactly," I replied. "The good news is that we have options, the first of which is moving a portion of your money into guaranteed income annuities. This would take some of the market exposure off the table and provide a bit more guarantee to your income strategy. However, that approach isn't without some downside for a man like you, who takes pride in having a $2,000,000 portfolio. You must understand it can't stay at that amount."

"For that reason," Karen added, "some people choose to go with cash value life insurance as a source for retirement income. While this approach has less market risk, it does still deplete the $2,000,000 asset. But you can more readily see the growth of the cash value, which gives clients the peace of mind of still having the asset."

Ted took a moment to collect his thoughts. "You're right. It's too risky to ask my money to play the role of two support pillars at once, and I think the best solution to my issue is to learn more about guaranteed income annuities. I like the idea of guarantees, even if that means I have to see a slightly smaller amount on my investment statements. How do I get that ball rolling?"

The best and worst part about financial planning is that there are so many options to select from; without appropriate guidance, this can be incredibly overwhelming. Thankfully, we were able to come to an agreement on the best approach for Ted's money—protecting a portion of the asset from market risk and creating guaranteed income for retirement—and that choice paid off well in the end.

However, there are less fortunate scenarios that no amount of planning can prepare for, and no amount of discussion can resolve. Ted hinted at such a scenario earlier—the Great Recession of 2008, 2009, and 2010.

The Great Recession
Case Study: John White

For this case study, I will be retelling a client meeting Karen had with John White. This occurred in 2009; I had just graduated college and was not quite in the business yet.

To this day, Karen vividly remembers this phone call from a desperate retiree who was watching his savings disappear daily.

Karen picked up the phone. "You've reached Stawicki Financial Strategies." (That was the name of her business when she was solo.) "How may I help you?"

"Hello, my name is John," our next client said. It was already evident in his tone that he was on edge and panic stricken. "I'm really hoping you can help me."

"Sure, John. What seems to be the problem?"

"Well, after twenty-five years of working for AT&T, I finally reached my goal of $2,000,000 in my 401(k) in 2006, so I submitted my paperwork for retirement. But now, only three years into retirement, my $2,000,000 is only worth $1,000,000. Its value has been cut in half. Can I even afford to be retired anymore?"

Karen could hear the total defeat in John's voice and asked him to do some math with her. She explained that while he was working and contributing, the down years of 2000 through 2003 hadn't had the same impact because he was still in the accumulation phase. However, once he retired, he was in the distribution phase, and the Great Recession of 2008–2009 (which was the worst economic downturn in the US since the Great Depression), combined with the income he was taking, had a completely different effect. Unfortunately, the math revealed he would have to either reduce what he was expecting from his retirement or go back to work for a few years. She briefly explained the strategy behind *The Power of 3* to help him understand the importance of minimizing risk.

"I wish I'd met you in 2007, Karen. If I had taken some of these risks off the table, I would have given my money permission to only do one job. Then maybe this wouldn't be happening to me."

"I know it's hard. But on the bright side, John, if we start planning and implementing the strategies from *The Power of 3* right away, you should be in a better place soon."

All too often, we meet people who have been told that if they work hard throughout their career and save enough money for retirement, they'll be fine. Unfortunately, this just isn't true. It's what you do with the money—how you allocate it—that creates a solid foundation for a successful retirement. And the biggest mistakes we see when we meet people for the first time is they don't understand the risks of putting their hard-earned money in one or two baskets or have failed to plan for a long life with guaranteed income to support their desired lifestyles. Unless they're like John and have been hit with a market downturn while in the Redzone, most of them don't have a clue that they are walking haphazardly across a minefield of risk. With some knowledge and planning, there is a better way—and it's much less stressful.

Chapter Wrap-Up

- Is longevity risk a concern of yours?
  - o   If so, what will you do to support yourself if long-term care is required later in life?
- Would you consider using the benefits of mortality credits by adding guaranteed income to your plan?
  - o   If so, what steps do you plan to take to get the ball rolling?
- What will you do to prepare for the Retirement Redzone?
- What can you do in advance to avoid an experience like John's during the Great Recession?

CHAPTER 3

CASH VALUE LIFE INSURANCE

T hey say only two things in life are certain: death and taxes. No matter who you are, where you live, or what you do, eventually, you will die. And worse, you will have to pay taxes not only throughout your life but after you die as well. (Well, your family will—at least on the remaining assets that are in taxable accounts.)

This brings us to our next subject: tax risk.

Tax Risk
Case Study: Sarah Monroe

Let's take a moment to talk about our client, Sarah. She was just starting her financial savings journey and, on the advice of her parents, sat down with us to get some direction now that she was in her first high-paying job.

"Thank you so much for taking the time to meet with me," she said, taking a seat in our meeting room one brisk winter morning. Sarah was just out of college and a year deep into her career as a human resources coordinator at a local hospital. "I'm sure I'm not like most of your clients because I'm just starting out, but I'm hoping you can give me some good advice, so I start my financial savings journey on a solid foundation."

"Sarah, this is exactly what we do," Karen replied. "Whether you've had years of savings and accumulated a lot of assets or are just in the beginning stage, our goal is to help our clients make smart financial decisions. So tell us a little about your goals."

"Well, my company has a great 401(k) plan, and they offer a match. Plus, my expenses are low right now, so I was thinking of contributing the full $22,500. I'm thinking this is a great idea because it will reduce my income taxes a lot."

The first place many people begin saving is in a 401(k). The advantage is that your contributions to a 401(k) are not declared as income, so you don't pay taxes on that money in the year you contribute. In addition, many employers match a portion of your contribution, which is essentially free money. This means for every dollar you contribute, your employer will also contribute a certain amount. The first rule of financial planning: *Take the free money!*

"Sarah, I love what you are thinking, and I am really happy to hear you say you want to save the full $22,500. However, I have to ask you a few questions," I interjected, taking out a notepad for reference. "Do you think this is the most income you are ever going to be making?"

Sarah scoffed. "I certainly hope not."

"How much of your contribution is matched?"

"50% of the first 6%."

"Okay, great. This is really helpful information." I jotted those numbers down on the notepad in front of me. "Do you understand that when you withdraw the money from your 401(k), after age 59.5—because that's currently when you can access it penalty free—your contributions and your employer's contributions will be taxed? If invested properly, both those amounts should grow to a significantly greater number than your original contribution, which sounds like a great plan until you realize you just grew more money for the government to tax."

"Wow." Sarah's eyes widened. "I hadn't really thought about it that way. I just always assumed that by adding more money to the 401(k), I'd have a larger amount when I could eventually access it."

"You're not wrong. The number in the 401(k) will, in fact, be larger, but it's not 100% yours. Remember, a 401(k), much like an IRA, might be called an individual retirement account, but they are really both joint accounts with the IRS, and, ultimately, the IRS is the one in control.

"This is what we refer to as tax risk. This is an easy trap to fall into because the concept of adding as much to your 401(k) as possible in one sitting in order to evade the annual income tax that is tagged to it seems like airtight logic. However, there is always fine print to be considered, which is why it can be hugely advantageous to work with a financial advisor." (Or to keep a book like this on hand, to brush up on the basics!)

"To put it as plainly as possible, the reason a large contribution to a 401(k) that is also matched to some level by an employer can be problematic is because we have no idea where taxes will be when you retire and want to access that money. Plus, since you didn't pay tax on your contribution or the match, it is 100% taxable when you take it out, at whatever the rate is at that time."

"Okay, Sam," Sarah said, looking a little alarmed. "Tell me there is a better way."

"I do have good news. What if I told you there was a way to pay your tax now and invest the money so it could grow for your benefit, and you'd never have to write a check to the government again? Well, there is—and it's called a Roth IRA, and for many companies who offer it, it's called a Roth 401(k)."

"Sign me up!"

Thankfully for Sarah, her 401(k) had a Roth option, so she was able to make her contributions to the Roth while her company match continued to go to the traditional 401(k). This meant that all her money would grow tax free to be accessed in the future. Her employer's contributions are still a traditional 401(k), so they get the benefit of the tax break today, but Sarah will have to pay the tax on this portion of the money when she makes her withdrawals in retirement.

However, when a Roth 401(k) is not an option, we recommend contributing what you need "up to the match" to get the contribution from your employer but then looking outside the 401(k) for tax-advantageous savings options, like cash value life insurance or Roth IRAs, which will be discussed further in this chapter.

The Seed or the Harvest

Many years ago, an important question was posed: Is it better to pay on the seed or on the harvest? The reason this question was so compelling was because it was considering the power of paying tax on one thing (the seed) capable of exponential growth rather than on the lump sum of something in its final stages of growth (the harvest).

It is our opinion that you should pay on both. We don't know where taxes will be in the future, and we don't know what the federal regulations will be, but we do know that half of any number will always be less than the whole of that number.

Paying on The Seed vs. The Harvest

We are now going to put our seed versus harvest analogy in perspective for you and show how it relates to your retirement savings. For this example, we are going to simplify our approach to the tax brackets. We will not focus on the complications of actual graduated taxes; instead, we will assume that 100% of income is taxed at your top income bracket.

If your income goal was $100,000 per year, it was taxable income, and your tax rate changed in retirement to 25%, you would pay $25,000 to the government to be able to spend $75,000. If that is your only option, it sounds pretty good.

However, what if you had two sources of income instead, each providing you with $50,000? The first source of income, like the $100,000 we just spoke of, is still 100% taxable when you are ready to access it. Therefore, at current rates, you would pay 15% on that $50,000, or $7,500, leaving you with $42,500 as income. But you already paid the taxes on the second source of income, meaning the whole $50,000 is yours to spend. If you take your spendable income from those two income sources, you now have a total of $92,500.

Would you rather have $75,000 because you had one source of income or $92,500 because you prepared and had two sources? (By the way, that is 23% more income you get to spend.)

The point is we don't know where tax rates are going to be in the future, but even if tax rates went up and $50,000 was taxed at 25%, you'd still have the other $50,000, which would be tax free, making your overall tax half as much as when all $100,000 was taxed at 25%.

I'll bet some of you have the same thought process as Sarah: "Wait a minute—if I pay the tax now, I will have less money to invest. That's why it's better to invest pretax dollars today and pay the taxes later."

9   "*The Power of 3* Masterclass." YouTube video, 14:55. Posted by Navigate Your Wealth, March 7, 2023. https://youtu.be/J4XWHhxvUCw

Many people believe that if they have less money to invest, they will have less growth in the end. It is not how much you have but how much you get to keep in the end that matters. To identify where you currently stand in the tax bracket system, refer to appendix A for a graph based on 2024 data. None of us can predict with absolute certainty where taxes will be when we retire, but there are a growing number who believe taxes are more likely to go up than down. Refer to the graphic below for a visual breakdown of how fluctuation in tax brackets when you get to retirement could ultimately leave you with less than if you had paid the tax from the beginning.

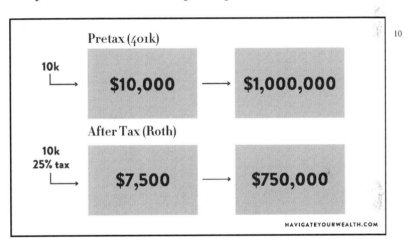

Let's assume we are comparing two investment options. The first is for a pretax contribution to go into your 401(k) for $10,000. This is the "paying on the harvest" scenario. The second investment—"paying on the seed"—will be an after-tax contribution to a Roth IRA for $7,500, with 25% saved for

10   "*The Power of 3* Masterclass." YouTube video, 16:37. Posted by Navigate Your Wealth, March 7, 2023. https://youtu.be/J4XWHhxvUCw

taxes. (We know this is higher than what you can contribute with today's limits, but go with us for a moment for ease of the example math.) Both accounts will grow at the exact same rate of return, and when you are ready to retire, with additional contributions and returns, the balances are now $1,000,000 in the 401(k) and $750,000 in the Roth IRA.

Which account has more money?

If you said the 401(k), you aren't looking at the whole picture. Remember, that 401(k) account is not yours—well, not entirely. The IRS hasn't taken their share yet. That is why we said unless the tax rates are lower than the 25% rate when you made the initial Roth contribution, the amount you will get after the IRS takes their cut could leave you with less than the $750,000 the Roth IRA has, which is 100% tax free and 100% yours.

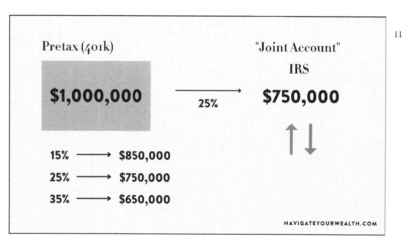

11   "The Power of 3 Masterclass." YouTube video, 17:44. Posted by Navigate Your Wealth, March 7, 2023. https://youtu.be/J4XWHhxvUCw

Can you imagine if taxes were actually *higher*—let's say 40%—when you retire? Your $1,000,000 investment would be worth only $600,000, which is significantly lower than the $750,000 in the Roth IRA account.

Something else to consider is that when—and, of course, if—tax rates go up in the future, how would a 20 or 30% increase in taxes affect your tax-free investment? The answer is that it wouldn't affect your investment at all. For this reason, we always encourage our clients to invest in the seed (or the Roth IRA) as well as the harvest (the 401[k] shared with the IRS).

Before we move on, it is important to take a look at where taxes have been in the past. No one likes paying taxes, but taxes are at historically low rates in 2024, as this book is being written and published. Again, no one knows where tax rates are going to be in the future, but it would be foolish to not identify that we have national debt that is currently through the roof and a government that won't stop spending. It seems clear that the only way to fix the problem is by going to the people.

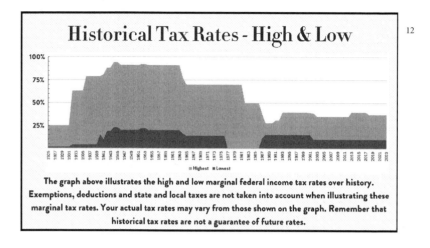

The graph above illustrates the high and low marginal federal income tax rates over history. Exemptions, deductions and state and local taxes are not taken into account when illustrating these marginal tax rates. Your actual tax rates may vary from those shown on the graph. Remember that historical tax rates are not a guarantee of future rates.

Generating Tax-Free Income

By now, you should be able to see the need for both taxable and tax-free income in retirement. Again, we fully endorse investing in not only the seed but also the harvest. However, income is much more likely to be taxed than it is to be tax free, so let's discuss how to generate and acquire tax-free income in the first place.

There are only three ways to get tax-free income:

1. Roth IRAs
2. Tax-free municipal bonds
3. Cash value life insurance

---

12   "Historical US Federal Individual Income Tax Rates & Brackets, 1862–2021," Tax Foundation, August 24, 2021, taxfoundation.org/data/all/federal/historical-income-tax-rates-brackets/.

Roth IRAs

Roth IRAs have certainly had their time in the spotlight in the last few years; some companies even include a Roth option for your 401(k) contributions, as we just saw was the case for Sarah.

13

The Roth IRA was established in 1997 and named for Senator William Roth (R-Delaware), who introduced it. A Roth is simply an individual retirement account that you contribute to with after-tax dollars. There's no current tax benefit, but your contributions and earnings can grow tax free, and you can withdraw them 100% tax free after age 59.5. (Once the account has been open for five years, you can access the funds up to your contribution amount.)

While the idea of creating the tax-free income in a Roth is great, there are limitations. The first is access to your

---

13   "William Roth" Wikipedia. Last edited on 26 February 2024. https://en.wikipedia.org/wiki/William_Roth

account—you don't have access to the gains until after age 59.5. As with an IRA, there is a penalty for accessing that money before a certain age. (Again, in this case, that age is 59.5 years.)

Additionally, there are universal contribution limits. For 2024, this limit was $7,000 per income earner ($8,000 if you are over 50 years old). But there are also earned income limits. So if you make too much money (currently, if your modified adjusted gross income [MAGI] is $161,000 for a single filer and $240,000 for married partners filing jointly[14]), you don't qualify for making Roth contributions at all.

We get it—paying even 20% to 30% in taxes feels awful, but what if when you get to retirement, your tax bracket is now at 40% or 50%? This is another reason we encourage our clients to prepare for the worst, and investing in both taxable and tax-free income is the safest way to do exactly that. This is why it has become so popular for people to invest in Roth IRAs and 401(k)s simultaneously over the years. By doing so, they are setting themselves up for more spendable income at the end of the day.

Three reasons Roth accounts are a great option to consider:

- You are looking for tax-free income in the future, and you do not need access to the money before you turn 59.5.
- You do not qualify or you do not have the funds required for cash value life insurance.
- You want the flexibility to contribute to a tax-free account but do not want to be committed to an annual premium/contribution amount.

---

[14] "2024 Tax Brackets," Tax Foundation, November 9, 2023, https://tax-foundation.org/data/all/federal/2024-tax-brackets/.

Let's say you do need access to the money prior to age 59.5, as that can be a real limitation to Roth IRAs. In that case, consider tax-free municipal bonds or cash value life insurance.

Tax-Free Municipal Bonds

There is a time and place for tax-free municipal bonds in an individual's portfolio, but this is the least commonly used strategy to create tax-free income. These can be thought of as loans that investors make to local governments and are used to fund public works such as parks, libraries, bridges, roads, and other infrastructure. Interest paid on municipal bonds is tax free (if they are bonds from your state and you are in a state that has a state income tax), making them an attractive investment option for individuals in high tax brackets. Plus, highly rated municipal bonds are generally very safe compared to almost any other investment.

However, it is important to also point out some of the disadvantages of munis. If you receive Social Security, your bond interest will be counted as income in calculating the taxable amount of your Social Security income. That could increase the amount you owe. Additionally, as with any bond, there is interest rate risk. If your money is tied up for ten or twenty years and interest rates rise, you'll be stuck with a poor performer, and the bond will lose value. Finally, although, as we stated, highly rated municipal bonds are generally safe investments, we have seen some of those bonds downgraded in their rating in the last decade as a result of financial issues in the municipality.

Three reasons munis are a great option to consider:

- For those who do not qualify for a Roth or cash value life insurance, they are a good tax-free option.
- They are generally a safe investment.
- If you live in a state with no state income tax, you are not restricted to purchasing bonds from your state. Ultimately, you can look at rates in all fifty states to select an option that works best for your individual scenario.

Cash Value Life Insurance

Now that we have discussed Roth IRAs and tax-free municipal bonds, we turn to another option in the realm of generating tax-free income: cash value life insurance, which is, in our opinion, the true knight in shining armor.

We have briefly discussed cash value life insurance already, but we will delve more deeply into the way it provides tax-free income in the following case studies, so be sure to stick around. And if you feel suspicious of life insurance in general, know you're not alone. Karen wasn't always a fan of life insurance either. She thought it was all smoke and mirrors and was convinced the only people who got rich in the whole scheme were the insurance companies.

Karen's career started in the investment world. She knew what she could do for her clients, and she was confident in her abilities and the ability of the market, over time, to go up. So she didn't need an outside insurance company taking away her clients' assets. This philosophy carried over into her career as a financial advisor, but after more thoroughly researching the back end of cash value life insurance and the value it could add to a client's portfolio, she eventually had to accept that she'd had it all wrong. It turns out that cash value life insurance is one of the very best ways to generate tax-free income. (Actually, it makes everything in your portfolio better.)

Term vs Permanent Insurance

Term insurance is designed to last for a specific, pre-set period, its only purpose being the death benefit. Permanent insurance, however, is designed to last your entire lifetime and, in addition to the death benefit, has living benefits included—one of which is the cash value.

The biggest difference most people perceive between the two is cost. For example, let's say term insurance costs you $1, and permanent insurance costs you $10. With this cost difference, most people ask, "Why pay more for something you won't be alive to enjoy anyway?"

The thing to understand is that term insurance is like renting your death benefit, whereas, permanent insurance is owning it. The reason someone might decide to rent their death benefit rather than own it outright is they simply do not have the premium needed to purchase a permanent policy. As you can see, this can be helpful if you are at the beginning of your savings journey, and you are looking to build over time. However, again, you are only renting the death benefit, and you're foregoing the option of living benefits, such as cash value. This is why term insurance is the cheaper option.

In almost every case, we recommend clients own permanent insurance. Yes, it is more money up front, but it also builds cash value, ultimately giving you access to those premium dollars.

Now, there is a time to rent. When you first got out of college, you probably didn't run out and buy a house. You needed to put a roof over your head. Term insurance does precisely that. It provides that death benefit, which will finance the chosen beneficiary upon your death and ensure they are taken care of, whereas permanent insurance will provide the very same death benefit but also allow you to build equity. Just like in owning a home, the equity goes to you instead of your landlord.

According to a Penn State University study, 99% of all term policies never pay out a claim. We've heard that statistic so many times, and every time we hear it, it feels just as absurd. The truth is, most people either cancel their term policies or let them expire after ten or twenty years. In fact, because of the increased cost of a term policy at the end of the designated time period, most people can't afford to keep those policies, even if they want to.

It's important to think about the word *cost*. We said before that term is cheaper than permanent insurance (permanent policies cost, on average, five to fifteen times more than term coverage with the same death benefit), but in reality, that only includes the initial out-of-pocket expense. If the premium is going to be costly either way, why not go with the option that has a better long-term payoff? Again, only 1% of people see the death benefit of their term insurance. That means there is a 99% chance you will invest in those monthly premiums for nothing in return. With a permanent policy, you have the ability to spend down your death benefit during your life and still have a 100% chance of leaving something behind. What we are saying is this: you need to think of your cost, not your out-of-pocket expense, in the bigger picture.

However, we don't expect you to just take our word for it. So, to better understand how life insurance works, we invite you to join us for our meeting with Brian.

Life Insurance
Case Study: Brian McDillon

There are really only two types of life insurance: term and permanent. The case study for this section follows 32-year-old Brian McDillon, who was interested in maximum coverage through a new life insurance policy. But, as with most things in finance, there is a lot to consider, and rarely is it as easy as it sounds like it should be. Let's dive in.

We met Brian when he was in his early 30s. We sat down with him in the early afternoon of a fall day. A friend of his had just had a baby and had recently gotten life insurance, but as he was describing the benefits to Brian, it led Brian to wonder if life insurance was something he too could benefit from having.

"Thanks for meeting with me today," he said with a smile, taking a seat in our meeting room.

"Of course, Brian. Let's dive right in," replied Karen, who was seated beside me. "You're interested in some guidance on life insurance?"

"Yeah," he said. "I just turned 32, and I'm realizing that I won't be getting any younger or healthier than I am now. A friend of mine recently got permanent life insurance, and it really put all this on my radar for the first time."

"So you've never had a life insurance policy before?" I asked, jotting down notes. Brian shook his head to indicate no, he hadn't. "How much would you say you know about life insurance? Do you have anything in mind, as far as what you'd like to get out of it?"

Brian looked a little sheepish. "Honestly, until a few weeks ago, I thought it just financed my wife if I die prematurely."

"Certain insurance types and policies will, of course," Karen interjected. "But there are also other types of insurance that will function as both a financial safety net for your beneficiary and a tax-free investment account."

"Yes, that is what my buddy was trying to tell me," Brian stated with a little chuckle in his voice. "But between you and me, he didn't do a great job of explaining how that actually works. I suppose before I get ahead of myself, though, I should ask about the maximum amount of insurance I can qualify for."

"At your age, the amount you can qualify for is typically around twenty times your annual income," Karen replied. "Your age does affect that coverage, however, and so do a few other factors, but that equation produces a reliable ballpark sum. This is often referred to as human life value."

"Can we ask about your annual income, Brian?" I asked.

"I'm making $250,000 a year," he replied. "But that's before taxes. Does that matter?"

"Actually, we want the pretax amount because taxes are ever changing; your gross income is how we calculate your maximum death benefit amount," I went on, jotting down numbers and preparing to do the math. "With that in mind, your projected coverage would be around $5,000,000—$250,000 times twenty."

Human Life Value

Do you value your life enough?

When it comes to the topic of life insurance, it's not uncommon to feel a sense of unease. After all, no one likes to think about their mortality, and the idea of calculating the value of human life can seem cold and clinical. However, understanding the concept of human life value can actually be quite helpful and even empowering.

So what exactly is human life value, and how do insurance companies determine it? Simply put, it's the present value of all the future earnings a person would expect to create for their family over their lifetime. This value takes into account a person's age, occupation, and income, as well as inflation and a discount factor.

While this concept may seem purely financial in nature, it actually has a very practical application. If a person were to pass away, their family would be left without their income, which could significantly affect their financial stability. By calculating a person's human life value, insurance companies can determine how much life insurance they can offer that person to ensure their family is adequately protected in case of their unexpected death.

But why can't a person be worth more dead than alive? The answer is quite simple: it would create a perverse incentive for people to harm or even kill themselves, which is obviously not something anyone wants. Additionally, from a practical standpoint, a person who is alive and healthy can continue to earn income for their family for many years. In contrast, a person who has passed away cannot.

It's worth noting that while life insurance may seem like a purely financial decision, it actually has very real emotional implications. Losing a loved one is always difficult, but knowing they have left behind a financial safety net can provide some comfort during a trying time.

So why is it important for you to understand your own human life value? For starters, it can help you make informed decisions about life insurance and financial planning. If you know how much you are worth in terms of your future earning potential, you can make sure you have adequate coverage to protect your loved ones in case something unexpected happens.

Furthermore, understanding one's human life value can provide peace of mind. While no one can predict the future, having a clear understanding of one's financial situation can help reduce anxiety and stress. It can also help individuals make smarter decisions about their finances since they have a clear picture of their earning potential.

Take a deep breath, think about your own human life value, and know that understanding this concept can provide both financial security and peace of mind.

"Great, I would love that level of coverage," Brian replied, "but how do I know if I want permanent or term insurance?"

"My guess is you will need a combination of both," Karen answered, and Brian's brows rose yet again with surprise. "I bet you didn't think you could do both, but you can. If our goal is to cover your full human life value—which is the maximum coverage you can receive from life insurance—then it is very likely we could be looking at a monthly premium that is more than what you can realistically keep up with if we made it 100% permanent."

"How high a monthly premium are we talking?"

"Probably somewhere around $50,000 a year," I said, circling the figure in my notes for reference. "That is 20% of your gross wages, which we want you to be saving. We don't want it all to go into one asset."

"That is a lot," Brian agreed. "Definitely more than I can afford with all the other places I'm saving."

"Which is why we suggest doing both term and permanent life insurance," Karen went on, picking up where she left off. "To help offset the cost of your monthly premiums, we would make a portion of the coverage permanent so you can build the cash value, but the remainder of the $5,000,000 would be in term coverage to provide adequate protection."

"But if I have some portion of it in term, it will eventually go away, right?"

"It might, if that's how we design it. But it is also possible to convert term policies to permanent policies in the future as your income grows or as your discretionary income increases. We call this the rent to own program."

"I had no idea that was even possible," Brian said, smiling at Karen.

Karen nodded. "This is called a term conversion. Approaching life insurance with this perspective is usually the way to go because all the premiums you are putting into the term ultimately go toward your benefit instead of the insurance company's."

Brian loved the idea. We ended up creating the right combination of both term and permanent, and over the next five years, we evaluated his income and converted a little bit of the term each year into permanent insurance. He felt good about this approach, but then life happened, and there was a medical factor that prevented Brian from ever qualifying for any more insurance. Thankfully, he already had all the term insurance and, thus, the death benefit he needed for his family in place. The good news is, with certain companies, you do not need to requalify for term conversions from a health perspective. This is why it is advantageous to get as much coverage as you can from the start. This gave Brain the option to convert his existing term policies into permanent policies, regardless of his health, to ensure his family would never be without that death benefit.

Remember, if your life changes, the cost also changes. For Brain, the upfront cost of the monthly premium was too expensive for him to go with 100% permanent life insurance initially, but when his diagnosis made his uninsurable, the opportunity to invest in permanent insurance became a priority for his family. With this in mind, Brian made sure he was able to convert what he could. He realized that if he hadn't initially gotten all that term insurance, he wouldn't have had access to the protection and cash value afforded by permanent insurance. That is why, when looking at insurance, you must have a big-picture perspective.

Think about it—when you purchase a home, homeowner's insurance is required. Most people opt for the homeowner's insurance to provide full replacement. If you have a four-bedroom house and your house burns down, you want the entire house rebuilt, right? You wouldn't be happy with a two-bedroom house instead.

Just like with homeowner's insurance, our client was seeking full replacement value with his life insurance. Through the combination of both term and permanent insurance, he protected his family for their short- and long-term goals. In doing so, Brian assigned his money one of the three primary jobs in *The Power of 3*—liquidity through cash value.

In fact, the best part of a permanent life insurance policy is the cash value, which, when designed properly, is like a Roth IRA on steroids.

Love it when a plan comes together, don't you?

Three reasons cash value life insurance is a great option to consider:

- The first reason we recommend a cash value life insurance policy as a Roth alternative is access. Unlike Roth, there is no age limit as to when you can access the cash value in your policy. For each premium payment you make, a portion of the money goes to the death benefit coverage, and a portion goes to build your cash value. As soon as there is cash value in the policy, it is yours, and, when accessed properly, it is 100% tax free.

- The second reason we recommend cash value life insurance is that it is a great alternative to a Roth IRA for a variety of reasons—the biggest being there are no universal contribution limits. The limit is strictly based on the amount of coverage you can qualify for. Since the death benefit and premium are directly correlated, the higher the death benefit, the higher the premium you can contribute. By design, in most cases, the premium can be significantly greater than the Roth contribution limits, ultimately giving you greater access to tax-free income.

- The third reason we so highly recommend cash value life insurance is the protection benefit. Now, let us be clear: in our *Power of 3* strategy, the value of life insurance comes from its living benefits. But if we are making an apples-to-apples comparison of these two tax-free options, it wouldn't be fair to ignore life insurance's greatest strength. What happens when the unexpected happens? Long-term care, chronic disease care, critical access, and, ultimately, the death benefit are things you don't have with a Roth. Most permanent insurance policies have free riders that cover these things, but even if that was not included, the death benefit would be greater than whatever the value of the Roth would be. It's how the policies are designed—your death benefit is always greater than your cash value.

The best time to get life insurance is before you need it.

Our goal is to be as transparent as possible so you walk away educated and ready to take action. It would be unfair of us not to point out two concerns most people have when it comes to life insurance. The first is how to qualify. To acquire life insurance, you must qualify, and that is based on health. So the younger and healthier you are, the lower the cost of the insurance. This means the best time to get life insurance is before you need it. But don't worry. Even if you are reading this and your 20s are well in the past, it is not too late. Through strategic reallocation of assets, we can make the increased cost of life insurance manageable.

Speaking of cost, this is the second concern people have around life insurance. They believe that since life insurance actually costs something while a Roth IRA does not, and a Roth IRA is more likely to grow to a larger value, that life insurance is more costly. Theoretically, that could be true. But there are factors that cannot be calculated on a guaranteed basis with a Roth IRA that make that statement more challenging to quantify.

For example, could Roth investments go down in value at any point during the scenario? If they are in the stock market, they sure could—whereas with our chosen options for life insurance, it can never decrease in value. But assuming the rate of return was the same and neither account went down in value, because of the unique way you can take money out of life insurance (even with the Roth IRA having a greater value initially), the total withdrawals from the life insurance would far exceed the total withdrawals from the Roth. This is a unique feature called arbitrage, which enables the policy owner to leverage income to enhance the growth potential of their cash value.

Don't believe us? We'd be happy to personalize it for you.

Sometimes in life, we need to give ourselves permission to do something we're uncomfortable with, and opting for cash value life insurance may be one of those things. Think about it— that death benefit gives you permission to consume your wealth differently. Now, instead of worrying about running out of assets or choosing a joint payout on your guaranteed income, you can make choices to increase your spendable income while you are alive, knowing that when you pass, your life insurance death benefit will replace what may have otherwise been exhausted.

Before we close out this chapter, we want to give you one more hypothetical story to better illustrate the importance of evaluating human life value. Once upon a time, a family was driving home from a fun day out. They were happy, chatting, and enjoying the ride when suddenly, a beer truck ran a red light and crashed into their car. Unfortunately, the father of the family didn't make it, but his wife and children survived, devastated and heartbroken.

The family knew they needed help, so they hired a personal injury attorney to represent them in court. They were seeking $5 million in damages for the loss of their beloved husband and father. The case went to trial, and after much deliberation, the jury decided to award the family $4.5 million based on the loss of income and future earnings. However, the judge delivered a shocking blow. The father only had $250,000 of life insurance in place, so the judge informed the family that since he had only valued his life at $250,000 while he was alive, that was all the judge could honor.

The good news is this can't actually happen, but it makes you stop to think. If the man had choked on a chicken bone at lunch, he believed $250,000 would take care of his family, but the jury believed $4.5 million was the right number based on his human life value.

We hope you can see how this story demonstrates the need for the proper amount of coverage from a protection perspective. But let's change the story. Let's say there was no car accident, the father didn't die, and he did get the proper amount of coverage. By funding this strategy, he would be able to create tax-free income and the liquidity he needed to fill that job description, and, on top of that, he could have his other assets fully invested in the market because the cash value in his life insurance worked as a bond alternative. (This is a concept we will expand on further in the next chapter.)

Chapter Wrap-Up:

- To maximize your income in retirement, you must address your future tax risk today.
- There are only three ways to create tax-free income:
  o Tax-free municipal bonds
  o Roth IRAs
  o Cash value life insurance
- The presence of a death benefit on the day you die gives you permission to spend your other assets differently in retirement.
- When purchasing life insurance, you should consider your human life value.

Finally, consider these questions:

- What is your strategy for creating/maximizing liquid assets?
- Will you have tax-free income in retirement?
- Have you insured your human life value?
- Can you spend your life insurance death benefit during your life?
- Do you have "permission" to spend down your assets?

CHAPTER 4

INVESTABLE ASSETS

N ow that we've talked at length about the first two compo-
nents of our *Power of 3* model, let's talk about the third
pillar—growth. This can look like investable assets, such as
stocks, bonds, and real estate, or essentially anything that can be
invested and fluctuates in value. Whether you use mutual funds
or hire a wealth manager to have an ongoing portfolio, one thing
is for sure—the market has a way of always outpacing inflation
(given enough time), and that's one of the risks that needs to be
protected against throughout your retirement years.

Market risk is the risk of your investments losing value as
a result of changes in the stock market. When you are working and contributing to a retirement plan, fluctuations in the
market may have less of an impact on your overall retirement
savings because you have time to ride out the ups and downs of
the market. However, when you are in retirement and relying
on your investments to provide income, market volatility can
be more concerning.

If you experience a significant market downturn early in
your retirement, your investment portfolio may be unable to

fully recover, leading to a reduced income stream for the rest of your retirement. In some cases, you may need to withdraw more money from your savings to cover expenses during times of market volatility, which can further erode your savings and potentially leave you in a precarious financial situation.

With *The Power of 3*, we help our clients take what would otherwise be a risk they thought they should eliminate or reduce in retirement (the stock market) and once again give them permission to be fully invested.

Remember when you were younger and the idea of being invested in the stock market was exciting? That was because you were in the accumulation phase, when you were saving money for the future. What makes being in the stock market too risky in retirement is when you need the money, and the market just took a big hit. That fear of not having the money when you need it or want it prevents so many people from staying invested, and ultimately, they miss out on the potential to maximize those dollars that the stock market offers.

Market Risk and Guaranteed Income Annuities Case Study: Kelly and Kevin Blake

This feels like a good time to introduce you to Kelly and Kevin Blake. These clients came to us through a seminar, so they had a basic understanding of *The Power of 3*.

"Sam, thank you for meeting with us today," Kevin had said at our first meeting. He and his wife shook my hand in turn before moving to do the same with Karen. The four of us sat in our usual conference room, and I poured them both a glass of water. "We are about ten years away from retirement, and we've saved in our 401(k)s over the years, but if we're being honest, we just have no idea if we have enough."

"No problem—that's really common," I answered. "First question: Do you know where all your money is? I know that might be a silly question, but most people just stuff old statements in drawers and expect to figure it out when they get to retirement."

Kevin smiled guiltily. "Well, you aren't far off. We've both worked for multiple companies over the years, and because we didn't know what else to do with it, we just left the money sitting in the 401(k)s we had through our employers; I think between the two of us, we have six or eight separate 401(k) accounts. Was that a bad strategy?"

"No, it's not bad, but it probably isn't working as hard for you as it could be. Plus, you left the companies—shouldn't you have taken your money with you?"

"Sure, but what could we have done with it?"

"Well, with any 401(k), you can roll it over into an IRA," Karen chimed in. "In an IRA, you control the investment options, and there are no tax implications for the rollover. Plus, in your case, you could consolidate all the old 401(k)s into one account, so it is easier to track."

Kelly and Kevin went on to do just that. They found all the old 401(k) statements and over the next month rolled their accounts into two separate IRAs. However, this was only the first step of the plan. Once they had all their money rolled into their individual accounts, they realized that because they had all of their money invested in the market—which is capricious and largely unpredictable—they were fully exposed to market risk. Once they saw the money consolidated, they realized their portfolios were invested like they were in their 30s and 40s, instead of in the home stretch before retirement. After hearing about this risk at the seminar, they scheduled a follow-up meeting with Karen and me.

"Sam," Kelly said at our follow-up appointment, "we just aren't risky people. Relying exclusively on the market isn't something we're comfortable with. Do you think that now would be a good time to move our money out of the stock market and into bonds so it's safe?"

"You are definitely on the right track with that line of thinking, Kelly, but I want you to think back to 2022. The Fed was raising interest rates in an effort to slow down the economy, which caused bond values to fall. Don't forget those things typically have an indirect correlation. When one rises, the other falls. As we stated, this doesn't happen often, but it needs to be planned for.

"In this case, the stock market also took a hit. This meant that the safe strategy of investing in bonds really backfired for so many people, meaning there was no safe place to hide."

"Wow, I just always assumed bonds were safe. So are you telling us we have to stay exposed to market risk?"

"Absolutely not," Karen reassured her. "This is a great time to introduce guaranteed income annuities into your retirement strategy. Our first step is to determine what your guaranteed expenses will be in retirement. Then we will use a portion of your IRA account balances and make sure we are covering your guaranteed expenses with guaranteed income; remember, these ultimately come from Social Security, pensions, and these annuities. Once you know your income is covered every month, you have permission to be fully invested in the market with your remaining IRAs."

"What do you mean by permission?"

"Well, since we know that your monthly expenses will be covered, you won't need to take money out of the market during a down year or quarter to pay for them. This means that you get to invest like you are in your 30s again—with time on your side—and truly take advantage of the principles of the market, such as growth and keeping pace with inflation."

As discussed in chapter 2, if you have enough guaranteed income to cover your basic needs, this will come from Social Security, pension—if you are lucky enough to have one—or guaranteed income annuities; you should never need to sell your investments to cover any of your basic expenses when the market isn't cooperating.

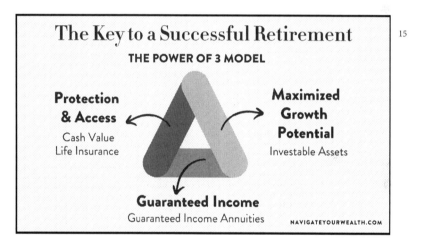

The Key to a Successful Retirement [15]

THE POWER OF 3 MODEL

Protection & Access
Cash Value
Life Insurance

Maximized Growth Potential
Investable Assets

Guaranteed Income
Guaranteed Income Annuities

NAVIGATEYOURWEALTH.COM

See how this is all coming full circle?

Additionally, with cash value life insurance, you have access to tax-free income when you might need something extra in

[15] "*The Power of 3* Masterclass." YouTube video, 27:38. Posted by Navigate Your Wealth, March 7, 2023. https://youtu.be/J4XWHhxvUCw

retirement. So the money in the market can remain invested as if you weren't going to touch it for a long time.

If you were planning for a big family vacation and expecting to pay for it with your stock investments, but the market decides to go down at the wrong time, don't cancel your vacation; take the money from the cash value in the life insurance, go on the trip, make the memories, take the photos, and when you return, be patient.

The market always comes back eventually, and when it does, you can sell what stocks you need and then put the money back into the cash value life insurance for the next time you might need it.

Our clients tell us with this modeling in place, they have the confidence to turn on the news and know that nothing can upset their apple cart. They have the income they need to enjoy retirement, the access and protection for emergencies, and the ability to continue to grow and keep up with inflation.

Will history repeat itself?

If most retirees aren't sleeping well, it's typically because the markets are in turmoil. In 2021, we witnessed the worst start to the stock market since the Great Depression and the second-worst start to the stock market *ever*. Additionally, 2022 encountered the first war in Europe in over seventy years, and we also experienced the worst bond market since 1982.

Furthermore, inflation is also a significant concern. Is inflation caused by all the aforementioned factors or vice versa? While there's certainly some cause and effect at play, government spending isn't helping matters.

In the '80s and '90s, it was more fun to be in the investment business because the market only went up (with the only exception being the largest drop in history in October 1987—which is just another testimony to how unpredictable the market can be). However, in 2000, the tech bubble burst, and the market dropped significantly. This was followed by the devastating 9/11 attacks in 2001, leading to another terrible market in 2002. This period of negative growth only lasted three years, but if you retired at the end of 1999 or the start of 2000, those first three years would have completely wrecked your plan.

From 2003 through 2006, the market began to recover, but then in 2008, the real estate bubble burst, leading to another severe market downturn.

In short, the market fluctuates up and down, and the question of whether history repeats itself remains. Planning and preparing for these cycles is essential to protect your investments, especially if you're nearing retirement age.

Market Risk and Your Retirement

If you're saving for retirement, you're used to seeing the value of your accounts go up and down with the financial markets. However, once you get to retirement, market volatility is a greater concern if you take withdrawals from your retirement accounts when they have declined in value, which may have a more significant long-term impact.

The following example illustrates this problem: Dan retires with a $1,000,000 retirement account and over the next twenty-three years, his account will have the same returns as the S&P 500 from 2000 through 2022.[16] For this example, we'll ignore the impact of income taxes and investment expenses, which Dan would have to pay if this were an actual investment. The average annual return over this twenty-three-year period was 5.9%.

Let's see what would happen if Dan decided to take $50,000 out of his retirement account at the start of each year. It seems reasonable to take a 5% withdrawal if the average has been 5.9%, doesn't it? But with this withdrawal strategy, Dan will run out of money in the fifteenth year of his retirement. Because the first three years produced negative returns (we just talked about 2000–2003), the portfolio can never recover.

Let's assume that we were in control of the order of his returns, and Dan was lucky enough to reverse the order—meaning they would run backward from 2022 to 2000. Not only would Dan have been able to take $50,000 per year, but he would still have $1,221,561 in his account in year 23, as shown in the charts on page 76-77.

We hope the charts "Dan 2000 - 2022" and "Dan 2022 - 2000" on the next two pages demonstrates why the average rate of return means nothing when you are withdrawing funds. It's the order of those returns—or what we call sequence of returns—that matters. The sequence of returns is critical, understanding your risk tolerance is critical—it's all critical.

Many financial advisors believe that the best way to help their clients is simply to create the biggest bag of money possible.

---

16   S&P 500 Historical Annual Returns 2010–2024, MacroTrends, https://www.macrotrends.net/2526/sp-500-historical-annual-returns.

But we have learned over the years that the guy with the biggest bag doesn't always win.

You see, assets can be lost, swindled, or simply consumed. The most valuable approach for our clients is offered through *The Power of 3*: guaranteed income annuities, cash value life insurance, and investable assets. Through this process, you have clearly assigned a job description for each dollar and allowed each dollar to work as hard for you as you worked for it.

Dan 2000-2022

Year	Beg. Of Year Acct. Value	End Of Year Acct. Value	Earnings Rate
2000	$1,000,000	$898,600	-10.14%
2001	$848,600	$737,942	-13.04
2002	$687,942	$527,170	-23.37%
2003	$477,170	$603,047	26.38%
2004	$553,047	$602,766	8.99%
2005	$552,766	$569,349	3.00%
2006	$519,349	$590,085	13.62%
2007	$540,085	$559,150	3.53%
2008	$509,150	$313,178	-38.49%
2009	$263,178	$324,893	23.45%
2010	$274,893	$310,025	12.78%
2011	$260,025	$260,025	0.00%
2012	$210,025	$238,189	13.41%
2013	$188,189	$243,893	29.60%
2014	$193,893	$215,978	11.39%
2015	$165,978	$164,766	-0.73%
2016	$114,766	$125,715	9.54%
2017	$75,715	$90,419	19.42%
2018	$40,419	$37,897	-6.24%
2019	-$12,102.00	-$15,598.00	28.88%
2020	-$65,598.00	-$76,264.00	16.26%
2021	-$126,264.00	-$160,217.00	26.89%
2022	-$210,217.00	-$169,350.00	-19.44%

For illustration purposes only. The results presented above do not represent any actual investment performance or the actual accounts of any investors.

Dan 2022-2000

Year	Beg. Of Year Acct. Value	End Of Year Acct. Value	Earnings Rate
2022	$1,000,000	$805,600	-19.44%
2021	$755,600	$958,780	26.89%
2020	$908,780	$1,056,548	16.26%
2019	$1,006,548	$1,297,239	28.88%
2018	$1,247,239	$1,169,412	-6.24%
2017	$1,119,412	$1,336,801	19.42%
2016	$1,286,801	$1,409,562	9.54%
2015	$1,359,562	$1,349,637	-0.73%
2014	$1,299,637	$1,447,666	11.39%
2013	$1,397,666	$1,811,376	29.60%
2012	$1,761,376	$1,997,576	13.41%
2011	$1,947,576	$1,947,576	0.00%
2010	$1,897,576	$2,140,086	12.78%
2009	$2,090,086	$2,580,212	23.45%
2008	$2,530,212	$1,556,333	-38.49%
2007	$1,506,333	$1,559,507	3.53%
2006	$1,509,507	$1,715,102	13.62%
2005	$1,665,102	$1,715,055	3.00%
2004	$1,665,055	$1,814,743	8.99%
2003	$1,764,743	$2,230,282	26.38%
2002	$2,180,282	$1,670,750	-23.37%
2001	$1,620,750	$1,409,404	-13.04%
2000	$1,359,404	$1,221,561	-10.14%

For illustration purposes only. The results presented above do not represent any actual investment performance or the actual accounts of any investors. [17]

---

[17]   "Solving The Retirement Puzzle" PowerPoint Presentation. Sequence of Returns, S&P 500 Year 2000–2022. Created March 2023. https://www.macrotrends.net/2526/sp-500-historical-annual-returns

Chapter Wrap-Up:

- Avoiding market risk is greater than just moving assets into bond portfolios.
- You must stay invested in the market to keep pace with inflation.
- History may not repeat itself exactly, but you should be prepared for it anyway.
- Accumulation and distribution need to be treated differently.
- The order of your returns matters in retirement.

Finally, consider these questions:

- Do you know your risk tolerance?
- Is your retirement strategy capable of keeping up with inflation?
- Can your invested assets withstand drastic market corrections?
- Is your distribution strategy for market investments different than it was during accumulation?

I have permission to remain invested in the stock market because . . .

CHAPTER 5

THINK OUTSIDE THE BOX

A t the beginning of the book, we promised to share some unconventional strategies for creating a successful retirement. With our *Power of 3* model, you are now considering solutions you may have previously overlooked or been advised to ignore. But we want to share one more strategy that our clients love, and it has to do with Social Security.

Conventional wisdom states that you should wait as long as possible before applying for Social Security, but is that really the best advice? We're sure you've heard people talking about Social Security and the best age to take it a hundred times, but this should not be a one-size-fits-all conversation.

There are a number of factors you need to consider when making this important decision. We're going to look at each of them now. First, you need to ask yourself, "Do I need the money?" For those of us who have not put together a well-rounded retirement portfolio but are on the cusp of retirement, the answer to that question is obvious: yes. For those of us who have compiled a well-rounded retirement portfolio, the answer may be a little less clear. Regardless of which group you're in, it's important to be realistic about where you stand financially. This is just one of the many reasons we argue this is not a one-size-fits-all discussion but rather something that should be handled on a case-by-case basis.

An important fact everybody needs to know is that each year you wait to access your Social Security money, your monthly amount increases by 8%. This makes for a pretty big incentive to wait to activate the benefit. However, perhaps the 8% increase isn't as important as financially supporting yourself sooner rather than later. Let's say you just turned 62 (which is the youngest you can be to access your Social Security funds) and ended up losing your job without warning. In this case, the interest generated from waiting to activate this benefit may not be worth it to you in the long run.

Most people, however, are justifiably enticed by that increase to the benefit amount. In fact, some people are so enticed that they wait too long and die before activating their benefit. This introduces a whole new round of questions, starting with what happens to your Social Security money if you die before accessing it.

If you're married, your spouse will get to keep whichever Social Security check is larger. So, if your check is larger than your spouse's, they're going to keep your check—but they're going to lose theirs. They will not get both checks. So keep that in mind. Also, it's not an investment account, so there is no contingent beneficiary. When you die, if you do not have a spouse, the IRS is going to keep that check.

Another thing to keep in mind is the fact that Social Security checks could be taxable, which means even though it is enticing to wait for that benefit amount to grow—and postpone your benefit for as long as possible—the longer you wait, the more taxes you may have to pay. This puts most of us in something of a predicament, which may be challenging to navigate without financial guidance. Good thing we're here, and good thing you picked up this book!

What if we could show you an out-of-the-box way to use that Social Security check while also lowering your taxes in the future?

The brilliant idea is to take Social Security early, when perhaps you don't need the income, and use it to pay the taxes on converting an IRA to a Roth IRA.

Confused? Stick with us.

We shared the importance of tax-free income in chapter 3. If you are nearing retirement, you might have a sizable IRA or 401(k) waiting for you, but it's still 100% taxable. We know that tax rates are historically low right now, so what if you were to capitalize on that by converting a portion of your IRA (which is that shared account with the IRS and thus taxable) to a Roth IRA (which is tax free)?

For those who don't need income from their retirement accounts, their plan is typically to defer the distribution until they are required to take it. This date is called their required beginning date (RBD), which is when required minimum distributions (RMDs) must be taken.

Would you be surprised to learn that if you took the value of your IRA and converted it over five years to a tax-free investment instead of simply taking the required distributions over the remainder of your lifetime (the RMD strategy), you would pay about a quarter of the taxes? Let that sink in for a second.

If it seems like the numbers don't add up, let us prove it. We'd be happy to run them for you. You can even run the numbers for yourself at www.NavigateYourTaxes.com.

Now most people do not have a huge chunk of money sitting off to the side, waiting to pay those taxes. So join us in our meeting with George Pierson to learn how we build out this strategy.

Let the Government Pay Your Taxes
Case Study: George Pierson

When our long-term client George Pierson was five years away from retirement, he booked a meeting with Karen and me to discuss his strategy. He had built up his portfolio with invested IRAs and stocks, had a robust cash value life insurance policy, and had a portion of his expenses in retirement covered with guaranteed income—the perfect *Power of 3* model. He knew once he retired, he would convert the remaining 401(k) into guaranteed income to fully cover his guaranteed expenses. However, he still had concerns. At the time, George was 65 years old and thus eligible to take Social Security, but he'd always believed that since he didn't need it, he would wait until 70 to start the income. Already, as we sat together in our office's conference room, I had a feeling that George, being the smart and disciplined man he was, might have fallen into the trap of foregoing his Social Security for as long as possible. And I was right.

"I just got my recent Social Security statement in the mail," he started off with, pulling out a few notes and his reading glasses, "and I just wanted to check to make sure that continuing to delay my benefit was the best strategy—you know, for that increased 8%."

"In your case, delaying is a good strategy at this point in time," Karen said. "You're still working, and you are under 67 years old, which is your full retirement age, so if you started collecting your Social Security income now, the government would withhold $1 for every $2 of earned income above $22,320 until the year you reach full retirement age."

"Excellent," George replied, closing his notebook and preparing to leave.

"Well, that's where I want to stop you," I interjected, and George slowly sank back into his seat. "While it is 8%, inflation was 8.7% in 2023, which means you would have gotten a higher bump if you had turned on the income."

George's gray brows furrowed. "I didn't realize that . . ."

"Now, if we start Social Security as soon as you reach retirement age, you could use the funds to convert some of your IRA into Roth IRAs, lowering your overall taxes in retirement. No, you wouldn't be getting that additional 8%—but with the potential cost of living increase you get once you turn on the income, you might not be making that much of a bonus, anyway."

"I love the idea of lowering my taxes. I just figured I was at the mercy of the government since I never started Roths all those years ago."

"Our goal would be to have you convert your IRAs into Roths over a five-year period because we want to take advantage of the graduated tax brackets, which would allow that money and any future growth on those converted dollars to be 100% tax free. Based on the math, you will end up paying about a quarter of the total tax. This means that what you save in taxes more than makes up for what you missed out on in your 8% bump in the years when inflation isn't so high."

"So basically, you are telling me the government will give me a check—my Social Security—and I'll use it to pay them off so I never have to pay taxes again?"

"You got it."

"Wow! This is a strategy I can get behind. But I can't start until I'm 67 years old, right?"

"In order for this to work successfully, you want to make sure you have reached full retirement age, or you are no longer working. Want to quit working now?"

We all shared a laugh, and George said, "Only if the numbers work."

Is your mind blown yet? That's the idea. But at this point, you're probably also wondering why we are giving you all this for free. Completely fair. At the heart of it, this is crucial information that we truly, deeply believe shouldn't be a secret. If we are being completely honest, this is just the tip of the iceberg when it comes to what's in our arsenal and what we provide for our clients. At the end of the day, we want you to know how straightforward and effective *The Power of 3* is. It shouldn't be locked behind closed doors, only available to certain people.

Penny Wise and Pound Foolish

Let's face it, paying taxes at any age is not fun, and at any rate, it's never good. Whatever amount you have to pay always feels like it's too much, regardless of the size. This is why when we have the opportunity not to pay any more than we have to, we should jump on it.

Your IRA or your 401(k) contribution is a perfect example of this. We'll bet at least once in your life, your accountant has said, "Did you know if you made an IRA contribution, we could lower your taxes?" That is not a lie—but it isn't the whole story either.

Yes, you will lower your taxes today, but the taxman is coming, and he's always going to get his due. And with your help, it's going to be a much bigger amount in the future because it's going to grow.

You may be thinking, *Wait a minute . . . I'm gonna be in a lower tax bracket when I retire, so I know I'll pay less taxes if I wait.* Who said that? Did someone put it in writing or give you a promise or guarantee that you're going to be in a lower tax bracket when you retire, or do you just believe that because someone said it?

Well, for those in their 20s or 30s, you have very little chance of ever being in a lower tax bracket. Seriously. How do we know that? Well, think about it. Are you not going to earn more over your lifetime as you climb the ladder of success? You're not going to be happy earning less than you are now when you retire.

Maybe you're looking at retirement thinking, *I won't need that much, so I'm going to be reporting less income in retirement, and that will drop me a bracket or two, right?* Well, let's look at a couple of facts you may not be considering.

First of all, today, I'm guessing you work all week and spend money on Saturday and Sunday, right? That's when most people spend the most money. You go to dinner, see a show, play golf, and take one, two, or three vacations a year. Well, here's a news flash for you: when you retire, every day is Saturday and Sunday. You've worked your whole life to be able to enjoy those retirement years and traveling, not sitting around the house watching game shows. You want to make sure you can enjoy them. That means you'll have to afford a lifestyle in which you spend money every day, not just on the weekends.

We mentioned earlier that tax rates are currently among the lowest they've ever been in history. In 1980, the top marginal tax bracket was actually 70%.

You heard that right, 70%! A married couple earning $100,000 a year was in the 59% tax bracket. They did what you're doing—funded everything they could to lower their taxes—and it worked. Today, they're actually pulling the money out at a lower rate. Those tax-deferred dollars from their 401(k) s and IRAs are only being taxed now at 25% to 37%. They're still complaining, but it worked.

Well, what do you think the chances of this working for you are? Candidly, our national debt escalates with each passing day, the government remains unable to rein in its expenditures, and the human lifespan continues to lengthen while the retirement age stays unaltered. The only way to fix this is either to get our government to stop spending or to raise taxes. Which one do you think is more likely to happen?

Earlier, we discussed our perspective on investing in both the seed and the harvest, and in situations like this, that philosophy still applies. Is it better to focus on what you'll pay in a single year or over the course of your lifetime?

Remember when we told you it was possible to pay a quarter of your total lifetime tax? Look at the analysis that follows in the chart titled "Potential Tax Impact" to better understand how that's possible for a 65 year old male.

Potential Tax Impact[1]
Current Pre-Tax Qualified Account $1,195,476

The values below show two scenarios:

(1) The total taxes paid if you live to age 90, assuming you continue to keep your qualified account, take RMDs when required, and reinvest these RMDs in a taxable account

(2) The total taxes paid if you live to age 90, assuming you roll over your qualified account to a tax-free account today, accounting for additional taxes during a conversion period.

Keep Qualified Account		Re-allocate to Tax-Free *	
Total taxes paid on RMDs at time of withdrawals	$374,907	Taxes paid on conversion	$320,384
Taxes paid on reinvested RMDs **	$122,251	Taxes paid on account growth	$0
Taxes paid on remaining account value at death	$449,079	Taxes paid on remaining account value at death:	$0
TOTAL TAXES PAID:	$946,237		$320,384

For the purpose of this report, the tax-free vehicle is assumed to be a Roth IRA.

*Tax-free accounts, like Roth IRAs and 401(k)s, have specific sets of rules and limitations. Please consult a qualified professional about your individual situation. This report is not intended to be a complete discussion of any qualified or tax free account or approach. This hypothetical example does not consider every product or feature of tax-deferred accounts or Roth accounts and is for illustrative purposes only. It should not be deemed a representation of past or future results, and is no guarantee of return or future performance. Your tax bracket may be lower or higher in retirement, unlike this hypothetical example.
**These materials are for informational purposes only and are not intended to provide tax, accounting or investment advice. Be sure to consult qualified professionals about your individual situation.
**RMD calculation data gathered from Stonewood RMD calculation software based on IRS guidelines and tables, and is hypothetical only. Your actual RMDs are determined by a variety of factors.

Because of the increasing value of the IRA over your life-time, increasing the RMD amount, and reinvested assets, the total tax burden grows for the government's benefit, not your own.

---

[18] "Could Your Tax Bill in Retirement Be Too Big? Compass Financial, www.NavigateYourTaxes.com.

Look at the two numbers at the bottom of each column in the chart. The difference is optional. You heard that right—by choosing to keep the qualified account, you are opting to pay more tax than necessary. The solution might be to bite the bullet, pay your taxes today, invest your money in tax-free vehicles; then, when taxes go up in the future, your tax on tax-free income will be zero. It's an absolute round number—zero.

Okay, let's get back to taxes in the future. As we said, the first rule of financial planning is to take the free money. So if your employer provides a company match on your 401(k), you should gobble that up. You should contribute up to that point, but then you need to consider some tax-free options with the rest of your savings.

If that same 401(k) offers a 401(k) Roth option, you should put your contribution into the Roth side. The company is still going to put your match into the traditional side because they want the tax deduction today, and of course, both the growth and the initial contribution will eventually be taxable to you.

Contributing to Your 401(k)

This is important. You should only be contributing to that 401(k) up to the match. Outside that match, it would be best if you looked for other tax-free options.

Ed Slott, a CPA and nationally known speaker and author, has a lot to say on this subject. We do too, but he's got a few quotes we want to share with you.

SAMANTHA M. IRISH AND KAREN E. STAWICKI

> "The key to successful investing is to buy low and sell high; the same is true with taxes."[19]
>
> "Your deductions on your 401(k) contribution are, in effect, a loan from the government."[20]
>
> The key to successful investing and tax planning is to understand the opportunities available to you and to make informed decisions based on your individual circumstances. By buying low and selling high, both in investments and taxes, you can maximize your financial outcomes and achieve greater success in meeting your financial goals.

If you're wondering whether you should be concerned about rising taxes, buckle up. Here are six ways you could owe more in taxes in the future.

First, you could make more money, move into a higher tax bracket, and owe more of your income in taxes. This is easily the fastest way to owe more taxes. The second easiest way would be if the government chose to raise taxes, meaning you could make the same income but owe a larger percentage to the government. Remember, in 2018, Congress passed a tax reform that lowered tax brackets for many Americans. But those individual tax bracket adjustments sunset in 2025, meaning that unless

---

[19] Ed Slott, *The New Retirement Savings Time Bomb* (New York: Penguin Books, 2021).
[20] Slott, *The New Retirement Savings Time Bomb*.

89

Congress passes new legislation, tax brackets will go back to their previous levels in 2026.

When most people think about having to pay higher taxes, these two scenarios come to mind, but there are still four other ways taxes can increase. The third way is by changing tax deductions, and we saw this recently with the Tax Cuts and Jobs Act.[21] Today, if you are still paying on your home mortgage, you can deduct what you pay in interest from your taxable income.

In the past, you could deduct up to $1 million, but this recent change lowered that to $750,000 for a married couple and only $375,000 if you are single. But if that deduction wasn't available at all, your tax liability would be even higher.

The fourth way you might pay more taxes is by expanding taxes. That means making taxes cover more of your income or subjecting new things to taxes, like Social Security. Remember, Social Security used to be 100% tax free. Now, up to 85% of your Social Security income could be taxable.

The fifth way is through legislative changes. Some of you may be aware of legislation passed at the end of 2019 called the SECURE Act,[22] which reformed some aspects of retirement savings. The act made changes to several things, including the age at which retirees must take required minimum distributions (RMDs) from a qualified account. Previously, that age was 70.5 years, then it was increased to 72. Now, with

---

[21] "Tax Cuts and Jobs Act: A Comparison for Businesses, Internal Revenue Service, last modified December 19, 2023, https://www.irs.gov/newsroom/tax-cuts-and-jobs-act-a-comparison-for-businesses.

[22] "H.R.1994: Setting Every Community Up for Retirement Enhancement Act of 2019," Congress.gov, accessed December 29. 2022, https://www.congress.gov/bill/116th-congress/house-bill/1994/text.

SECURE 2.0, that age is 73 and is going up to 75. Legislation like this is just another way government regulations could affect your retirement savings.

Ultimately, your tax risk is up for election every two years.

The last way taxes could be higher in the future is what we like to call the widower's penalty. When a spouse dies, the surviving spouse now files as a single taxpayer. If their income has not decreased, they will likely find themselves in a significantly higher bracket. Talk about adding insult to injury!

Okay, enough of the doom and gloom of taxes; let's wrap this up.

Chapter Wrap-Up:

- When to activate your Social Security benefit is extremely personal, but waiting to get the 8% increase could ultimately cost you more.
- If you don't need the Social Security income immediately, consider using it to convert your IRAs to Roth IRAs to create more tax-free income in retirement.
- *Always* take the free money, but beyond that, consider other tax-free investment options outside your 401(k).
- There are six ways taxes could be higher in the future, most of which are completely out of your control. It's important to know what these are and prepare for the worst however you can.

Does your current financial strategy leave you paying more optional tax?

What is your total tax burden? (Visit www.NavigateYourTaxes.com to find out.)

CHAPTER 6

THE FINAL WRAP-UP

We have covered a lot of territory in *The Power of 3*, and you have plenty to digest, so let's do a final wrap-up to make sure we're all ending on the same page.

We started out by talking through the risks you may face in retirement and how, ultimately, the way to create a successful retirement is to eliminate those risks—which, shockingly enough, is entirely possible.

(Note: these principles work whether you've accumulated hundreds of thousands or millions. No matter where you are, this is a strategy designed to suit all.)

The first risk we eliminate is longevity risk, or the risk of living too long. Our goal is to ensure that for every guaranteed expense our clients have, they also have guaranteed income to cover it. We never want them to have to worry about what the stock market is doing, where rates are going, or how they will pay their bills this month if they decide to take an extra vacation.

Peace of mind creates wealth, and wealth creates successful retirements.

The next risk we covered was tax risk, or paying more tax over your lifetime than required. We took the time to explain that taxes could negatively affect your retirement future, but they don't have to.

Through the presence of cash value life insurance and other tax-free income options, you can be in control of how much you pay in taxes on an annual basis. If you are lucky, you will be retired for a very long time, which means that tax rates will most likely change over those years. But no matter what the tax rates are, you will have already planned ahead with cash value life insurance or Roth IRA conversions and can distribute your income to create the lowest possible tax burden each year.

We covered longevity risk through guaranteed income, ultimately fulfilling the job description of income you can never outlive. We addressed tax risk with tax-free options, which include cash value life insurance. The cash value of permanent life insurance satisfies the job description of liquidity.

The final risk addressed in our *Power of 3* model is inflation risk and the fear of missing out. We turned the market—an otherwise incredibly risky solution—into your permission slip to capture all the benefits. You now have permission to keep pace with inflation and stay fully invested to achieve maximum growth, which fills your money's third job description. You can now ride out the down years because if history repeats itself, the market will recover.

Remember, if you desire a successful retirement and want to turn the tables on conventional saving strategies, we are here to help. Creating better financial outcomes is not only what we do but also what our clients have come to expect from us.

As we've stated multiple times throughout this book, your money has specific job descriptions: to grow, to be liquid, and to provide income. When you ask one dollar to do more than one task, it can't properly do any of them. Through *The Power of 3* model, we have clearly defined the job descriptions of your money and given it the power to work optimally for you and your success.

We leave you with this last thought: "If what you thought to be true turned out not to be, when would you want to know it?"

---

23   Photography by Liz Schneider. www.lizschneiderphoto.com. Location: Schloss Solitude, Stuttgart, Baden-Württemberg

ARE YOU OUR CLIENT?

Y ou may be wondering, *Am I a good fit to work with Compass Financial?* Our ideal client is someone who seeks to pay the least amount of taxes that is legally possible. They strive to live a life of abundance and are motivated to take action. You must be coachable and want success for yourself and your family as much as we want it for you.

Examples of clients we serve:

- Individuals/couples who possess a million dollars or more in assets and are focused on minimizing their tax liability.
- Individuals/couples who own multiple retirement accounts and desire expert guidance to create maximum sustainable income to maintain their quality of life.
- Individuals/couples who are in the accumulation phase, earning a six-figure income, with the ability to save 20% of their gross wages annually, and are looking for a clear direction for those dollars.

If you identify with any of these, let's connect.

However, if you are still on your way to achieving significant financial milestones, do not be discouraged. We have courses, seminars, and workshops that you can attend to get you started on the right path.

Plus, if we've said it once, we've said it a million times—the best time to get started was yesterday!

As you've likely gathered, we refer to solutions that other advisers may have turned their noses up at, such as annuities and life insurance. However, when we talk about these policies, we're coming at it from a completely different angle. Our job is to prove to you with math and science just how powerful these financial tools are and how, when leveraged effectively, you can approach retirement confidently.

Whether this is your day one or one day, we are glad you're here and look forward to helping you take steps toward the lifestyle you want for yourself and your loved ones.

From ours to yours, welcome to the family.

GLOSSARY

- **Annuities:** Contracts between you and an insurance company that require the insurer to make payments to you, either immediately or in the future. You buy an annuity by making either a single payment or a series of payments.
- **Beneficiary:** The person or entity you legally designate to receive the benefits from your financial products.
- **Cash value life insurance:** Permanent life insurance in which a portion of each premium you pay goes toward insuring your life while the rest goes toward building up cash value.
- **Chronic disease care:** Rider that provides an acceleration of death benefits if the insured is certified as chronically ill. This rider can reduce the financial burden by helping pay for medical expenses and other costs related to chronic illness when the insured meets certain qualifications.
- **Contingent beneficiary:** The secondary beneficiary you designate, should the primary beneficiary be deceased at the time of your death.
- **Critical access:** Designed to help fill the financial gaps not covered by traditional health, disability, life, and accident insurance. If a life-threatening illness occurs, critical illness riders provide a benefit to help protect quality of life.

- **Death benefit:** The amount of money your insurer will pay out to your beneficiaries if you die while the policy is in force.
- **Full retirement age (FRA):** The age you must reach to receive full retirement benefits from Social Security. Your FRA varies depending on the year you were born. The FRA in the United States is 66 years and 2 months for those born in 1955, increasing gradually to 67 for those born in 1960 or later.
- **Guaranteed income annuity:** An income product that provides you with a monthly/annual income that is guaranteed for life, no matter how the markets perform.
- **Human life value (HLV):** A number insurance companies use that gives the present value of future income an individual might earn over their lifetime. The HLV number is used to determine how much money would be required to secure the lives of your dependents if you were no longer around.
- **Living benefits (of life insurance):** With these benefits, the cash value money can be used while the insured is still alive. For example, they can borrow against the cash value of the policy for emergencies or medical payments and even to supplement their retirement income. The cash value of the policy is the insured's to use as they wish.
- **Long-term care:** Services that include medical and non-medical care provided to people who are unable to perform the basic activities of daily living, such as dressing, toileting, transferring (getting in or out of bed or a chair), eating, bathing, and continence. Long-term support and services can be provided at home, in the community, in assisted-living facilities, or in nursing homes.

- **Monte Carlo analysis:** A mathematical technique that predicts the possible outcomes of an uncertain event.
- **Mortality credits:** "The secret sauce," also known as the mortality yield. With a participating annuity, premiums paid by those who die earlier than expected contribute to gains in the overall pool and provide a higher yield or credit to survivors than could be achieved through individual investments outside the pool.
- **Required beginning date (RBD):** The official date by which a retirement account plan owner must begin taking required minimum distributions (RMDs) from their accounts.
- **Required minimum distributions (RMDs):** Minimum amounts that IRA and retirement plan account owners generally must withdraw annually, starting with the year in which they reach age 72 (73 if they reached age 72 after December 31, 2022).
- **Retirement Redzone:** The five years before and the five years after retirement. Poor market performance during this period can have serious effects on your portfolio.
- **Roth IRAs:** Individual retirement accounts to which you contribute after-tax dollars. While there are no current-year tax benefits, your contributions and earnings can grow tax free, and you can withdraw them tax free and penalty free after age 59.5 once the account has been open for five years.
- **Tax-free municipal bonds:** Interest income from municipal bonds is exempt from federal income tax. In addition, municipal bonds issued in your state may be exempt from state and local taxes.

APPENDIX A

2024 Tax Brackets and Federal Income Tax Rates [24]			
Tax Rate	For Single Filers	For Married Individuals Filing Joint Returns	For Heads of Households
10%	$0 to $11,600	$0 to $23,200	$0 to $16,550
12%	$11,600 to $47,150	$23,200 to $94,300	$16,550 to $63,100
22%	$47,150 to $100,525	$94,300 to $201,050	$63,100 to $100,500
24%	$100,525 to $191,950	$201,050 to $383,900	$100,500 to $191,950
32%	$191,950 to $243,725	$383,900 to $487,450	$191,950 to $243,700
35%	$243,725 to $609,350	$487,450 to $731,200	$243,700 to $609,350
37%	$609,350 or more	$731,200 or more	$609,350 or more

---

[24]   "2024 Tax Brackets," Tax Foundation.

REFERENCES FOR FURTHER STUDY

Reading Recommendations

Hegna, Tom. *Paychecks and Playchecks: Retirement Solutions For Life*. Maricopa, AZ: TDH Financial Enterprises, LLC, 2011.

Kelly, Patrick. *Tax-Free Retirement*. Victoria, BC : Trafford, 2007.

McKnight, David. *The Power of Zero, Revised and Updated: How to Get to the 0% Tax Bracket and Transform Your Retirement*. Crown Currency; Revised, Updated edition (September 4, 2018).

Ruby, Martin H. *The New Rules of Retirement: The Risks No One Is Telling You About . . . And How to Fix Them*. Louisville, KY: Martin H. Ruby/Stonewood Financial Solutions, 2016.

Ruby, Martin H. *The No-Compromise Retirement Plan: Overcoming the Compromises in Your IRA to Live a Happier Retirement*. Louisville, KY: Martin H. Ruby/Stonewood Financial Solutions, 2018.

Slott, Ed. *The New Retirement Savings Time Bomb: How to Take Financial Control, Avoid Unnecessary Taxes, and Combat the Latest Threats to Your Retirement Savings*. New York: Penguin, 2021.

Watch Our YouTube Videos

https://www.youtube.com/@navigateyourwealth

Get Your Retirement Tax Bill

www.NavigateYourTaxes.com

Schedule a Consultation

https://calendly.com/navigateyourwealth

LIFETIME FINANCIAL ORGANIZER

Organize yourself for the next major life event

Key Contacts	Office Phone	Cell Phone
Financial Advisor Name:		
CPA/Accountant Name:		
Attorney Name:		

General Items	Location
The following general documents should always be readily available.	
Adoption Papers	
Birth Certificates	
Driver's License	
Marriage/Domestic Partnership/ Civil Union Certificate	
Passport/Citizenship Papers	
Prenuptial	

Safe & Combination	
Safety Deposit Box and Keys	
Separation or Divorce Papers	
Social Security Card	

Emergency Papers & Information	Location
The items below may be needed when someone becomes seriously ill.	
Living Will/Health-Care Proxy	
Durable Power of Attorney	
Financial Institution's Propriety Power of Attorney	
Beneficiary Forms for IRA, 401(k), or other Benefit Plans	
The items below may be needed soon after someone dies.	
Cemetery Plot Deed	
Charitable Donation Preference(s)	
Burial Instructions	
Death Certificate	
Funeral Home Preferences and Information	
Information for Obituaries	
Last Will and Testament	
Letter of Instruction from Deceased to his/her Executor/Executrix	
Military Discharge Papers	
Phone Number/Address of County Surrogate Court	
Prepaid Cremation Documents	

Life Insurance, Annuities & Other Insurance Policies	Location
Life Insurance policies as well as any variable or fixed annuity document needed to settle claims.	
Group Life Policies	
Health and Accident Insurance ID Cards and Claim Records	
Life Insurance Policy Documents	
Mortgage Insurance Policy	
Travel Insurance Policy	
Variable Annuity of Fixed Annuity Statements/Documents	
Beneficiary Forms for Insurance and/or Annuity Policies	
Long-Term Care Insurance Policy	
Property and Casualty Policy Documents	
Veteran Administration Insurance Papers	

Financial, Bank & Credit Documents	Location
Documents needed to settle outstanding credit accounts and debts, free up necessary cash to settle the affairs of an estate, and transfer ownership per last will and testament.	
Appraisal or Inventory of Valuable Items	
Buy/Sell or Partnership Agreements	
Certificates of Deposit (CDs)	

Checks and Checking or Money Market Account Statements	
Credit Card and Account Statements	
Credit Union Account Books or Statements	
Deferred Compensation Agreement Documents	
Federal/State Gift-Tax Returns	
Lawsuit or Documents on Pending Legal Actions	
Loans Outstanding (Money Owed)	
Medical Bills, Prescription Plan Card/Records	
Mortgage Documents	
Motor Vehicle Title Papers	
Passbook Savings Accounts	
Prior Years' Tax Returns	
Promissory Notes (Debts Owed)	
Property and School Tax Records	
Real Estate Deeds, Other Titles of Ownership	
Rental and/or Lease Agreements	
Trust Documents/Agreements	

Investment Documents	Location
Documents needed for the transfer of ownership per last will and testament and credit applications.	
Alternative Investment Documents (Including K-1s)	
Bearer Bonds Not Held in an Account	
Beneficiary Forms for IRAs, 401ks, or Other Benefit Plans	
Company Retired Plan Statements from all Employers	
Documents Showing Cost Basis of Securities Owned and Sold	
Individual Retirement Plan Statements	
Investment Club Documents/Records	
Mutual Fund Account Statements	
Online Securities Transaction Information	
Other Company Benefits (e.g. Deferred Compensation)	
Stock Certificates Not Held in an Account	
529 College Savings Plans Statements	

NOTES

Made in United States
Orlando, FL
19 January 2025

57470633R00070